Favorite Dog Hikes

In and Around Los Angeles

By Wynne Benti

for my Dad xoxo Chomger

Spotted Dog Press, Inc. • www.SpottedDogPress.com

Spotted Dog Press, Inc.

www. SpottedDogPress.com

Published by Spotted Dog Press, Inc.
Bishop, California
We welcome your comments and ideas! Please write us at:
Spotted Dog Press, Inc.
Box 1538
Bishop, CA 93515
or e-mail us at spdogpress@qnet.com

Fourth Printing
1999

ISBN Number: 0-9647530-0-6

Photographs by author unless otherwise noted.
Cover photo: Andy Zdon & Spotted Dog Press CEO, Syd,
(an Australian Cattle Dog) check out Mt. Baldy from the
Big Horn Mine Trail by Wynne Benti
Back cover inset photo: the author in the Arroyo Seco by Rosalie Ammerman
Canine boot illustrations & design ©1995 by Terry Austin
Book design & layout by Spotted Dog Press, Inc.

Printed in the United States of America

Table of Contents

A Note About Safety

Various aspects of hiking, which include climbing mountains, have certain risks and hazards associated with them. Some of these hazards include, but are not limited to, adverse weather conditions, snake bites, insect bites, animal bites, dehydration, hypothermia, heat exhaustion, or other types of injury.
There is no substitute for experience, skill and knowledge of safety procedures.

The author and publisher of this guide make no representations as to the safety of any hiking or driving route described in this guide.
At the time of this printing, all route descriptions were accurate.
However, conditions are constantly changing and it is recommended that you contact the supervising park agency or consult available map information to find out about current conditions.

Acknowledgments

There are several people who provided information for this book and we would like to acknowledge them: the Santa Anita Small Animal Clinic whose excellent staff patiently answered various canine-related questions about health and hazards in the wilderness and who at various times patched up outdoor-related cuts and scrapes; the Arroyo Seco District Ranger Office of the Angeles National Forest who answered questions and provided printed materials about Angeles National Forest and wildlife-related issues; the Santa Monica Mountains National Recreation Area whose backcountry rangers answered questions concerning trail conditions; wild New Zealander Terry Austin, a fast-hiking dog lover, for his wonderful drawings and positive words of encouragement; Pete Yamagata from up north who shared his photographs with us around the desert campfire; Walt Wheelock whose inspirational climbing guides were the first ones we could afford to buy and who, years later, through various twists of fate, became our friend; Scot Jamison who brought little "Sadie" up into the mountains — the well-conditioned Pomeranian who enjoyed hiking the mountains and was quite good at it; Ruskie the rock climbing hound – what a sight it was to watch he and Ms. Julie Rush climb side by side on a third class section of Mopah Peak in the California desert; Charlotte Feitshans, Jo Solomon, Julie Sheer, and the whole K9 gang for their enthusiasm and determination to take dogs and people to the beautiful wild places of the west; Leo Cordell and Bruce Hale who were the first to show me that most trails were made for dogs; Rosie, Joseph, Patty, Breann, Edmund, Hien and Justin for being there; Andy Zdon, my dearest husband, who served as model extraordinaire for many of the photographs. We would also like to thank everyone who provides a good home to a homeless cat, dog or other companion pet. It doesn't take much for us to make the difference in their lives.

Introduction

In 1880, on an expedition to explore the southeastern part of Alaska, John Muir, the 19th century naturalist and wanderer of the west, discovered just how remarkable a companion a dog could be in the wild. On that expedition, despite Muir's objections, one of his traveling companions brought along a little dog named "Stickeen." The dog was exceedingly small and as far as the participants of that expedition were concerned, it couldn't possibly serve a useful purpose except to only get in the way of serious exploration and study.

But, as dogs often do, Stickeen surprised everyone on that great Alaskan expedition with his fortitude, courage and will. No storm was too fierce, no river current too fast, no mountain canyon or crag too treacherous to deter the little dog from walking along side his human companions.

During the early years of exploration in Alaska, dogs were as important a resource to those adventurers as horses were to the pioneers and frontiersmen of the old west. Dogs were team members on the very first explorations of the north and south poles. They pulled sleds and carried packs full of equipment. American aviator and explorer Admiral Richard E. Byrd, who organized and led many notable polar and transatlantic flights beginning around 1925 was the first man to fly over both the north and south poles. Accompanying Admiral Byrd on his polar flights was his small terrier "Igloo" who also shared notably in his master's accomplishments. Throughout history, dogs have been a valuable asset to their human companions as shepherds, protectors, workers and rescuers.

Our dogs, KD and Syd, have never made history, but they have always walked with us along the trail whenever or wherever we take them. They have walked with us through forests of pine, canyons of sycamores and oaks; to the summits of mountains, and along the trails of the coast and wind-blown grasslands. As soon as they hop out of the car and feel the dust of the trail beneath their paws, they intuitively know to start walking, and to keep on walking, until they reach the end of the canyon,or the top of the mountain. Like most dogs, our dogs love to explore, whether it be a new mountain trail or the old, familiar fire road not far from the house. They love the mountains and forests — the smell of the chaparral, the feel of the sun warming their fur as they nap atop the summit of a peak, or the taste of the cool water of a spring-fed stream as it gently cascades over gray boulders, through ferns and the bloom of late spring flowers.

When we put on our hiking boots, our dogs know that they will soon be leaving the backyard behind. It is impossible for them to contain their excitement. Though they won't be jumping over crevasses or navigating through Alaskan terrain like their canine ancestors, or searching for victims in the debris left behind by snowy avalanches or fallen buildings, they do share in our small adventures to the beautiful mountains, canyons and grasslands in and around Los Angeles.

This trail guide includes some of our favorite walks in and around Los Angeles, which we have done time and again with our dogs. In so many trail guides and books about hiking, dogs are mentioned as an afterthought, usually in the chapter about trail courtesy, the "no" chapter as we like to call it. The "no" chapter is the one about all of the "no" things, the things that you're not allowed to do — no littering, no smoking on trails, no radios, no motorized vehicles and no dogs. For someone who loves dogs, those "no" chapters helped inspire the writing of this book. Since most trail guides are written only for people, there's little information available about trails and parks in and around Los Angeles where dogs are welcome visitors.

Near the end of 1993, we began scouting walks for this book. KD, Syd, and my husband accompanied me on trails we had walked for years in the San Gabriel and Santa Monica Mountains. We also found some new trails such as those in Palo Comado Canyon, one of the newest additions to public parklands in southern California.

Before the book was finished, fires had swept across some of the most beautiful country in the Santa Monica and San Gabriel Mountains. After the fires, came floods and mudslides. Then, on January 17, 1994 a big earthquake hit Los Angeles, followed by even more floods, and a few more devastating wildfires.

Ironically, on the day we scouted the Latigo Canyon to Castro Crest hike via the Backbone Trail, a sizeable 5.3 aftershock swept over the Los Angeles basin. We were walking back down the trail from the oak-covered crest, when we ran into a terrified couple who asked:

"Did you feel the quake? It must have been a really big one. We were sitting down, having our lunch when we felt the ground shake beneath us and saw the mountains move up and down."

Contrary to their experience, we hadn't felt or seen a thing all day. The dogs never reacted, as far as we could tell, to the uplifting and downshifting of the land. They just happily roamed the trail, sniffing the flowers and other oddities. At home, they certainly were more sensitive to tremors, but then they weren't distracted by the many wonders of the trail. We could only conclude that during our downhill descent, we all must have been moving up and down, in perfect sync with the rolling of the mountains.

Perhaps the most valued contributors to all of this were KD and Syd, the two little furry characters adopted from the East Valley Animal Shelter in the San Fernando Valley. KD was adopted first — a skinny stray which had been picked up scrounging on the streets of Los Angeles, whose good-natured smile radiated from behind the cold steel bars of her cage. Little did we know that she would become a veritable hiking-machine, driven into a wild, lurching frenzy by the very spelling of the words "outside" or "walk."

When Syd was adopted a year later, she was on her final day of life. Had she not been adopted that day, she would have been put to sleep. Perhaps it was her unusual looks – a scruffy, spotted dog, that caught my attention. "I'll take her," I said to the attendant, who responded as he gently lifted the shy little pup from the cage saying, "This will be a loyal, good dog." On the way home through the foothills of the San Gabriel Mountains, she stood on the wheel-well of the truck with her head poised upward out the window. With her eyes closed, it seemed as if she was taking her last breath of freedom in a life which, up to that point, had undoubtedly been very hard on her.

Nine years later, KD is still obsessed with the word "walk" while Syd, the spotted dog, is content to spend her days sleeping in front of my office doorway.

The dogs are our companions for life, and without them, there would have been little inspiration to write this trail guide. It is our hope that everyone, dog and human alike who uses this book, has as much fun as we did walking the beautiful trails on our favorite dog hikes in and around Los Angeles.

"Mr. Young and the Indians were asleep,
and so, I hoped, was Stickeen;
but I had not gone a dozen rods before he left his bed
in the tent and came boring through the blast after me.
That a man should welcome storms for their
exhilarating music and motion,
and go forth to see God making landscapes
is reasonable enough;
but what fascination could there be in such
tremendous weather for a dog?"

John Muir, Stickeen: The Story of a Dog • 1909

"My burro and I, and a little dog,
are going on and on, until, sooner or later,
we reach the end of the horizon."

A letter to "Bill" from Everett Ruess,
traveling by foot across the southwest • 1931

1
The Essentials

This trail guide was written for anyone who wants to leave the city behind for a day, to hike the trails, or experience the mountains and valley grasslands in the company of their favorite dog. It is a guide to some of the prettiest and most natural parkland trails, in and around Los Angeles, where a dog is as welcome a visitor as a person. It is not a book about dog-training, nor does it pretend to be. There are a few basic suggestions throughout the text about equipment and supplies which, if not already known, will certainly contribute to making a day-hike more enjoyable for both dogs and people.

The hikes in this book have been walked and timed by two dogs — a slender, long-legged 40 pound Lab/Greyhound mix named KD and a stout, stoic, somewhat plump, short-legged 50 pound Australian Cattle Dog named "Syd." KD has big, tough paw pads, great physical endurance and a slender build which makes it easy for her to do hikes and mountain climbs that many dogs (and people) are unable to do. Syd, on the other hand, has small, delicate paws and a heavy build which makes it difficult for her to go long distances without a lot of physical conditioning and some kind of leather hiking boots on her paws.

Syd, KD, and many of their canine friends, have helped the author determine the ratings of difficulty for each hike. These ratings are based on "dog abilities," and can be adjusted to fit your dog. The more you hike with your dog, the more familiar you'll become with their hiking abilities and habits. Owners will also find, listed in the informational headings for each hike, minimum recommended water requirements for a medium-sized dog, based on moderate southern California temperatures. The more you hike with your dog, the better you'll be able to judge just how much water to carry for both of you. As a good rule of thumb, always carry a spare gallon of water in your car. If you underestimate the amount of water carried on a hike, you'll have a back-up in the car on your return. Many of the trailheads for the hikes listed in this book are quite a distance from any water source. Remember, water is the most essential item in both human and canine hiking gear.

At the time of this writing, dogs were, of course, permitted in all of the places listed in this book. Throughout southern California there are a large number of places where dogs are not allowed, leashed or unleashed outside of parking lots or campgrounds — most national parks and monuments, state wilderness areas including state parklands in the Santa Monica Mountains. "Adventure passes," which can be purchased from the USFS and other retailers, are now required for any visit to the Angeles National Forest.

Dogs are allowed, with few regulations on Bureau of Land Management (BLM) and United States Forest Service (USFS) lands, city and county lands and most national recreation areas which are supervised by the National Park Service, like the Santa Monica Mountains National Recreation Area. Most regulations in these areas concern the use of leashes and are usually posted at the park entrance or on backcountry use permits. If you ever have any questions, always call the supervising land agency before your planned trip.

MULTI-USE TRAILS:
SHARING THE TRAILS WITH OTHERS

As our trails have grown in popularity over the past decade, so have the ways in which people are using them. Today, dogs and their owners must share the trails with walkers, runners, hikers, mountain bikers, equestrians, packers and pack animals, fishermen, bird-watchers, hunters — people of all ages and interests.

Also include in that lengthy list of people all of the ones this author didn't think to mention as well as those people who like dogs, those who are afraid of dogs and those who don't like dogs. Knowing this, dog-owners have a great responsibility on and off the trail to always keep their four-legged hiking companions close to them, preferably by leash or by verbal command.

The most important verbal command you can teach your dog for wilderness travel is "come." When you shout your dog's name along with that word, your dog should forego all other distractions, and return to you at once. In fact, your dog's ability to respond to that one simple command could mean the difference between life and death. For many of us though, leashes are the best way to know where our pet is all the time. Leashes are valuable for many other reasons. They also help keep dogs from inadvertently stumbling upon and further investigating, rattlesnakes, for instance. If you want to let your dog enjoy the trails or get some exercise off-leash, you should always carry a good six-foot long leather leash so you can clip and un-clip as situations arise. Also, make sure your dog can turn on a dime when you give the command "come," regardless of any immediate or tempting distraction. Remember, keeping your dog leashed will keep your dog safe.

Just like people, all dogs have individual personalities. Their unique responses to situations along the trail may at times be difficult to predict, particularly if they are unleashed. Sometimes a dog's worst enemy on the trail, with the exception of rattlesnakes, ticks, and mountain bikes are other dogs, particularly those dogs which are not leashed or are not under their master's verbal control.

A word here about mountain bikers. There seem to be two types: mountain bikers who navigate the trails with care and concern for other trail-users, and those who seem to be oblivious to the presence of others. On more than one occasion, we have watched mountain bikers speed down a trail, not once reducing their forward momentum, even when they were within close range of people and dogs. A person, and especially a dog, wandering the trail could inadvertently wander into the path of a mountain bike. Dog owners need to be aware of this, particularly on the popular trails. The more you are aware of what's going on around you, the safer and happier you and your dog will be.

More often than not, you will meet up with other dogs along the trail who share your love of exploring wild places. Like people, dogs will come in an assortment of sizes, shapes and personalities, some friendly, some not so friendly. Eventually, you may even meet up with an "alpha" dog. An "alpha" must be the top dog above all others — the leader of the pack — and will fight until death, literally, to be the leader. Jack London wrote about the "alpha" behavior of sled dogs during the 1898 Klondike gold rush in his classic book, "The Call of the Wild."

My sister and her husband have a large Rottweiler named "Big Bart" who loves to go hiking with them. Big Bart is an "alpha" dog. If Big Bart was off-leash, his primordial instinct would direct him to dominate any other dog who might mistakenly cross his path. Actually, that's putting it very nicely. He's 120 pounds of "holy terror." His owners know what he's like, and they prefer not to impose his personality on others. So, whenever Big Bart is outside his own yard, walking the trails and enjoying the mountains, he is on a leash. This is not to say that all Rottweilers are like Big Bart. They are not. Any pure or mixed breed of dog has its share of alpha personalities.

Once, on an excursion to the Angeles Forest, we encountered a dog and his master in a trailhead parking lot. We had just parked our car when the dog saw our two hanging their heads out the window, and immediately rushed across the parking lot, while his master with arms a-flailing, yelled a litany of confusing, garbled commands. The beast leapt against our brand new car clawing the paint, and proceeded to get into a snarling, vicious rage while our two dogs responded in stunned silence. The owner's excuse for his dog's unruly behavior? He quickly attributed the nasty tantrum to the "protective nature" of the breed. Actually, it was more indicative of poor training and the inability of the owner to teach his dog that one simple, but important command — "come."

Many of the dogs you'll meet along the trail would probably rather sniff the flowers and smell the mountain air than have anything to do with mountain bikes, rattlesnakes or other dogs. Just the same, if you were to meet any of those things along the trail it's really nice to have the option of being able to reel your pet in with his or her leash.

One of the most important things for any owner to do, is to "socialize" his or her dog at an early age — get "Fido" used to being around other dogs. "Socializing"will help your dog feel comfortable around other canines and with a little obedience training thrown in, helps minimize aggressive behavior towards other dogs in later years.

Only you know your dog. With the knowledge you have of your pet, you should always be prepared to deal with any unexpected situation that might arise — everything from the presence of horses, children, mountain bikers, wildlife or other dogs along the trail. And remember, you might have to carry your dog if he or she becomes injured or too tired to walk back to the car.

TRAIL ACCESS

Every government agency — city, county, state or federal — that oversees public park lands, has its own set of rules concerning dogs, including but not limited to the use of leashes, owner control, and access to park lands. Usually, those regulations will be posted at the

Ruskie comtemplates the forbidden zone. (PHOTO: Julie Rush)

trailhead or indicated on the wilderness permit if one is needed.

Once, we drove almost three hours to hike with our dogs to the top of Suicide Rock in the San Jacinto Mountains near Palm Springs. We picked up our permit at the USFS office and were told that dogs were allowed on the trails. It was even written on the permit. We parked at the "signless" trailhead, under the jurisdiction of the California State Park System and started the hike. About a quarter mile up the trail, we were greeted by a big sign that stated "no dogs on trails." However, a mile or two up the same trail, where it crossed over into national forest land, dogs were allowed. So, it pays to call ahead if you're unsure about the regulations concerning dogs. There is nothing more frustrating then getting up at o'dark-thirty to pack for a full-day's excursion into the wilds with your dog, drive an hour or more to a trailhead, only to discover a big posted sign which states that dogs are not allowed on the trails. If an area permits dogs without leash, they usually require that the dog be under "voice command" control.

Ultimately, all owners need to realize thay they, and only they, are responsible for their dog's behavior on the trail and for knowing the rules concerning dogs for the particular area they'll be visiting.

Drinking out of a lightweight plastic container on Sandstone Peak.

WATER, LEASH AND A BOWL!

Water, a lightweight plastic bowl and a sturdy leash are essential items for owners to carry on any venture into the wilds with their canine companion. Water is the most important item to have with you on any hike — for both you and your dog.

Water weighs about 1-3/4 pounds per quart — something to remember if you're going to carry the water supply for both of you in your day pack. If you want your pet to carry its own water, you can purchase a dog pack from a good camping store. If you forget a bowl, a plastic lunch baggie can double as a make-shift bowl in a pinch.

Under the main heading for each hike listed in this book, is a recommendation for the minimum amount of water you should bring for your dog. The amounts recommended in this book were based on the needs of a medium-sized dog weighing about 45 pounds in moderate temperatures (65-70 degrees). Every dog is different and it will eventually be up to you to determine how much water your dog will need. It is good to always carry a container with extra water in your car. Large, collapsible plastic water containers (from 2-1/2 gallons on up) are available from outdoor equipment retailers. Following a hot, dusty hike, dogs welcome a long, wonderful drink of water back at the car.

Never depend on a natural water source such as a stream, for yours or your dog's water supply. Streams can be dry at any time of the year or unfit for human or canine consumption. Humans should never drink from any natural, unfiltered water source in the Santa Monica or San Gabriel Mountains, or any other wilderness location in the west — sad but true. Most streams in southern California contain bacteria and other contaminants which can cause various intestinal ailments. These ailments result in unpleasant symptoms such as adominal pain, gas, diarrhea or worse.

There is a particularly nasty protozoal parasite known as Giardia Lamblia. It originates from human and animal waste that gets into, and contaminates, water sources. The small giardia cysts, not visible to the human eye, can usually be removed from a water source with the use of a portable water filter, available from an outdoor equipment store. Portable water filters typically are used on extended backpacking trips when it's not convenient to carry the additional weight of bottled water or when not enough water can be carried for the duration of the trip.

Giardiasis is something you don't want to get. It can cause many disagreeable symptoms like acute adominal pain, severe intestinal gas and bloating, as well as recurrent diarrhea and vomiting that can last up to three to four weeks. Without immediate medical attention, people can end up in the hospital. Dogs can also get Giardiasis and other ailments from drinking contaminated water. If a dog becomes infected, the symptoms can include diarrhea and vomiting. If your dog displays these symptoms after drinking from a natural body of water, contact your vet immediately to obtain treatment. For the dayhikes listed in this book, the author recommends carrying all water.

WILDERNESS SANITATION

A word here about picking up the gifts (scat) your dog may leave behind. A large unsightly pile in the middle of the trail should be reason enough to want to dispose of it. However, perhaps the most important reason for cleaning up after your dog is to avoid contaminating wilderness water sources.

Some people advocate the use of a plastic trowel and a ziplock bag — to carry out any scat. Perhaps one of the better rules of good wilderness sanitation, and more practical, is to do what humans are supposed to do — dig a hole. Using your foot, a rock or a plastic trowel, kick or dig a hole, 6 – 8 inches deep and 8 – 10 inches wide, at least 200 feet from any water source. Place the scat in the hole. Fill the hole with the loose soil and tap the soil firmly back into place with your foot. As a last resort, if these options are not feasible, move the scat off the trail.

FIRST AID

A first aid kit for humans contains many items that can be readily used on a dog as well. A roll of 1" waterproof tape, some 2-1/4" x 3" medium adhesive pads and one or two rolls of gauze, can come in handy for taping sensitive paw pads. Include an anti-bacterial ointment like neosporine, which owners and dogs can share alike. A pair of tweezers are essential to any first-aid kit, especially for removing ticks or cactus spines. If your dog wears hiking booties to protect its paws, consider carrying a spare set just in case one is lost or torn.

A word here about evacuating your dog. We've not yet had to carry one of our dogs out of the back country, but we have watched other people do it. One fellow had to carry his dog on his shoulders, wrapped around his neck like a scarf. Others have loaded their dogs in their packs, which was fine, since the dogs were small enough to fit in the packs. If your dog gets sore paws, is injured or becomes too tired to walk back to the car, you'll have to be prepared to handle the situation. It's just something to know about. If you and your dog are in good condition and you're familiar with the terrain, the chances of this happening will be greatly reduced.

POISON OAK

This is a word for owners. On many of these trails, especially in the canyons, poison oak grows with a vengeance, from spring through the end of fall. Avoid touching it! If you do have an allergic reaction it usually appears in the form of a rash, up to a few days after initial contact. Depending on the severity of the reaction, calamine lotion or over-the-counter hydrocortisone cream helps relieve the itching. More severe outbreaks require a visit to the doctor. We knew a fellow who was on an extended backpack, days from a doctor's office or a pharmacy, when he discovered that the ridge he had just walked down was covered with poison oak. He happened to be near a stream, which he jumped into, completely washing himself down from head to toe. Either he wasn't allergic to the pesky flora or the washing worked, because he never got the rash associated with his exposure to that ridge covered with posion oak.

Though we've not ever known a dog to get poison oak, dogs like people, can be allergic to anything, including poison oak. Canine allergy symptoms include chewing of paws, scratching of sides and pawing at ears. It is very possible for humans to get poison oak by coming in contact with animal fur that has rubbed against poison oak. Several mountaineering medicine books currently on the market, have whole chapters dedicated to poison oak, its effects on people and the best way to treat it. Remember, whenever you have a question concerning poison oak, it is best to contact your physician or veterinarian.

HYPOTHERMIA

It is not possible to talk about all of the various potential hazards and risks facing both people and canines on the trail, but knowing about some of the most important ones can help you avoid them. One of these trail hazards is hypothermia, a particularly insidious condition caused by exposure to cold and moisture which, if ignored, can cause death. Hypothermia occurs when the body experiences heat loss. When this happens, the body's core temperature begins to drop, impairing brain and muscular functions.

There are a number of ways to get hypothermia. The most common way is not dressing warmly enough to insulate the body from adverse environmental elements including, but not limited to, exposure to cold temperatures, rain, snow, and wind. It is important to recognize the symptoms of hypothermia at the onset so that they can be treated quickly. Symptoms of mild hypothermia include: feeling very cold, numbness of skin, minor muscular impairment especially hand movement, and shivering. As the body temperature drops, the muscles seem increasingly uncoordinated, there is a slowness of pace, mild confusion, apathy and amnesia. In severe cases, inability to walk or stand, confusion, dilation of pupils, unconsciousness and eventually death.

Preventing hypothermia requires clothing, food, and water. Drink water to avoid dehydration. Eat snacks, high in carbohydrates, at frequent intervals to provide and restore energy supplies for physical activity and production of body heat. Most importantly, dress in layers. The first layer of clothing worn against the body, should be polyester or polypropylene long underwear, top and bottom. Forget cotton for thermal protection. When cotton gets wet it takes a very long time to dry. It just holds in cold and moisture. Cotton shorts and tee-shirts

Too tired to walk, Barbee gives Sadie a lift. (PHOTO: Pete Yamagata)

are great for summer hiking, but you should always carry a spare layer of "polypro" just in case your cotton gets wet. Over that, a wool or plush synthetic polyester sweater. Wool and polyester are the best insulators against cold and moisture. The third layer should be a waterproof, breatheable nylon rainjacket that can double as a windbreaker. The final critical item is a wool or polyester weave hat or balaclava, since a great amount of heat loss occurs at the head. Be sure to also include a pair of wool or synthetic gloves and socks. As conditions change, add or subtract layers. If a person comes down with hypothermia, warming them with another human body can be a life-saver. For instance, if a sleeping bag is handy, climbing in the sleeping bag with them can quickly help restore their body temperature.

Dogs can also fall victim to hypothermia, though their symptoms may not be as obvious. Once, we took a hike on Rock Creek in the Sierra Nevada with our dogs. Before we knew it, KD broke through a snowbank and fell into the fast-moving waters of the creek When we pulled her out, she was soaked to the bone. A winter storm was moving in, with dark gray clouds overhead and the wind blowing a fierce gale. She was shivering uncontrollably by the time we got to the car.

Since we always carry a spare towel in the car, we were able to dry up most of the water, though she was still quite damp. We turned the car heater on full blast, and she was still shivering. One of us got into the back of the car and held her, rubbing her down to warm her. With the warmth of a human body next to her and two big dog biscuits later, she finally stopped shivering.

HEAT EXHAUSTION

Heat exhaustion is the opposite of hypothermia, occurring when the body temperature goes up instead of down. There are a number of factors that can cause heat exhaustion. The two biggest are dehydration (not drinking enough water) and physical overexertion when it's too hot. Some of the symptoms of heat exhaustion include physical weakness, dizziness, nausea, vomiting and headache. As soon as symptoms are identified, the victim should sit or lie down, preferably with feet elevated. He or she should be moved out of direct sunlight if possible and given something to drink, preferably containing salt, and should not resume exercise until all body fluids are restored.

Heat, combined with overexertion can have detrimental effects on a dog, especially if the dog is dehydrated, out-of-shape or not used to the strains of hiking on a mountain trail. Canine symptoms of heat exhaustion and overexertion include vomiting (particularly after drinking), a stumbling gait, glassy or tired looking eyes. When we first began hiking with our dogs in the San Gabriel Mountains, Syd was really out of shape. Along the trail, she would run for shade and eventually would start vomiting. By the time we got back to the car, she was completely exhausted and moved at an exceptionally slow pace. We determined that her symptoms were a result of overexertion, heat, not drinking enough water, and quite possibly altitude. We solved this problem by opting for easier hikes until she was able to build up her physical endurance. We also carried more water and stopped more often for shorter water breaks.

RATTLESNAKES, TICKS & OTHER WILD CREATURES

At any given time during the year, rattlesnakes and ticks are part of the natural environment of the western mountain ranges, including the Santa Monica and San Gabriel Mountains. Rattlesnakes are about the best reason for owners to keep their dogs leashed, particularly during the spring and summer when rattlesnakes tend to be out and about in greater numbers. A rattlesnake bite can be quite deadly for a dog and access to medical attention must be immediate The best defense against rattlers is not to let your dog get bitten in the first place.

After every hike, owners should give their dogs a full-body tick check. Owners should run their hands through the dog's fur, from head to end of tail. Ticks feel like small, protruding moles and measure from an 1/8" to 1/2" depending on how long they've been attached. If a tick is found, use a pair of tweezers to pull it out. Simply, push the dog's hair away from the affected area. Place the tweezers closest to the point of tick contact with the dog nearest the tick's head (which is beneath the skin). Get a good firm grasp of the tick with the tweezers and pull it out, with firm force. Pull out any leftover tick parts with the tweezers, and clean the affected area with soap and water or some rubbing alcohol. If you ever have any questions, always contact your vet. On the trail, we carry pre-packaged alcohol pads which can be used to disinfect human and canine wounds. Owners should also give themselves a tick check especially if they've been hiking in terrain with brush and tall grasses.

Until recently, mountain lions were a very rare sight in the local Santa Monica or San Gabriel Mountains. During the first part of 1995, there were several documented physical encounters between lions, humans and dogs, mostly in the backyards of homes adjacent to the Angeles Forest. During the twenty years or so that we've hiked in the mountain ranges of southern California, we have never seen a bear and have only seen one mountain lion. He was roaming the barren hills above Leo Carillo State Beach, which had recently burned. We didn't bother him. He didn't bother us. He was more interested in a small herd of deer wandering about on the open ridge.

Even though the chance of being struck by lightning is greater than that of being attacked by a mountain lion, there are a few things to know about mountain lions. They are elusive, hunt mostly at night and prey upon large animals like deer, but can also survive on a diet of small animals. They most often ambush their prey from behind. Their attacks are quick and usually come without warning.

The California Department of Fish and Game publishes a handy pamphlet called "Living with California Mountain Lions" which is available at Angeles Forest Ranger offices or directly from Fish &

Signing the summit register.

Game headquarters at 1416 Ninth Street, Sacramento, CA 95814; (916) 653-7203. The pamphlet offers a few helpful pointers for dealing with mountain lions, most of which are common sense.

The first recommendation is not to hike alone, if possible. Keep children close to you (studies have shown that mountain lions are especially attracted to children). Don't approach a lion (if you meet up with one, try to give it a way to escape). Avoid running from a mountain lion (that will stimulate their instinct to chase). Try not to crouch or bend over (a person bending over or squatting looks like four-legged prey to a lion). Do all you can to appear larger (remain standing, raise your arms and wave them slowly while speaking in a firm, loud voice; throw stones, branches, whatever you get in your hands without turning your back or bending over). Fight back if attacked, remain standing and face the animal (people have fought them off successfully using rocks, sticks, garden tools, jackets and their bare hands).

Most importantly, for your dog's well-being and safety anytime you travel in a wilderness environment, keep your dog close to you and know where your dog is at all times. This is why park rangers stress the value of keeping your dog on a leash when hiking. A leash can save a dog's life in the wild!

THE HIKING ESSENTIALS

You will need a daypack to carry your food, water, first aid and other items necessary for an enjoyable day hike. Daypacks are available in varying sizes and weights for people and dogs. On day hikes, we carry water for us and our dogs. Depending on the hike, that usually means 2–3 liters of water. Two-liter plastic soda bottles are an inexpensive and lightweight water bottle solution. Your dog should have a collar with a license or some other form of identification.

It's really important to carry a few first aid items which can be used in a variety of different situations for both people and dogs. These items include a pair of tweezers (for removing ticks, splinters or spines), moleskin or waterproof tape and gauze (for protecting against or patching blisters or cut paws) and an anti-bacterial ointment.

You can try dog packs on dayhikes, though dogs seem to have more fun without them. Generally, dog packs are better for backpacking excursions where a couple of days will make a difference in the amount of weight carried. For people, the author recommends always carrying the items listed below, known as the ten essentials:

1. Map
2. Compass
3. Flashlight, spare batteries
4. Food and water
5. Clothing (lightweight rain jacket/pants that can also double as a windbreaker; wool or synthetic sweater)
6. Pocket knife
7. Matches in waterproof container
8. Sun glasses, sunscreen
9. Hat
10. First aid kit

A pair of comfortable hiking boots is a must. Boots that fit well are essential to the complete enjoyment of the outdoors. Walking for miles on blistered heels is not the most pleasant experience. Dogs paws are also sensitive to rough terrain. In fact, sore, cut or worn out paw pads are probably the most common reasons for having to carry a dog out of the backcountry. Making or buying a set of boots for your dog is a good way to avoid this problem. There are a number of canine boot styles on the market, some available from mail order catalogs specializing in pet products.

Tama models his canine boots. (PHOTO: Terry Austin)

Without exception, the best canine hiking boots are made from soft, pliable leather or suede.

After years of experimentation, a fellow hiker named Terry Austin discovered that he could make boots with relative ease for his Golden Retriever, Tama. Using suede, shoelaces and two simple tools, the boots Terry designed and made for Tama were a very practical solution for protecting his paws on rugged or rocky terrain and for long hikes.

Using the basic pattern, shown on the following pages (final size will vary depending on the size of your dog's paws), a set of four suede booties with spares, can be easily made for a reasonable cost. When you are ready to make the boots, first fit your dog with a sample, for size, cut from paper or cloth. This way, you should be able to get an exact fitting without expending any of your real materials. Nylon shoelaces are durable and seem to be the best material for longevity. They must be tied fairly tight around the paws so the boots don't slip or fall off.

How to Make Your Own Canine Hiking Boots

Materials needed: good quality suede leather, a hole-punching tool, an eye-riveting tool and 27" nylon shoelaces.

Using the pattern shown below, cut samples out of paper or fabric to determine sizing for all four paws. Trace pattern onto leather using a light color pencil. Cut the boot shape out of the leather. Punch holes for laces, front claws. Rivet holes for laces only. Lace shoelaces (use different colors for a stylish look) through holes, and presto! You have a new set of fine hiking boots for your canine companion!

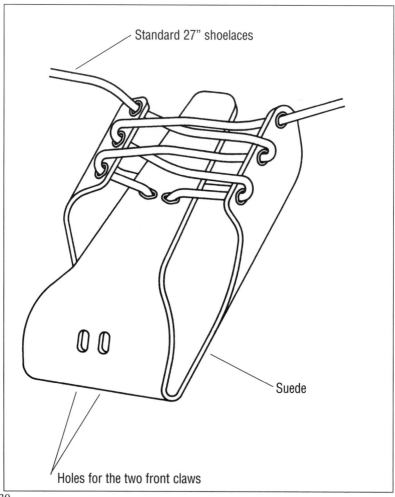

Standard 27" shoelaces

Suede

Holes for the two front claws

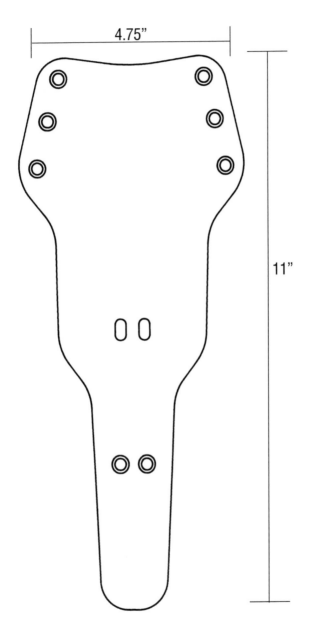

4.75"

11"

Dimensions shown on these pages are for larger dogs.
Customize lengths and widths to fit your dog's paws.
Drawings shown are not to size.

Design and drawings by Terry Austin.

Dog-friendly K9 Committee dayhike to climb Eagle and Antimony peaks in the Los Padres National Forest near Frazier Park.

HIKING WITH A GROUP

If you are thinking about hiking with your dog for the first time, and you would prefer to hike with a group, there are a number of groups that lead canine oriented hikes. One of these, the Sierra Club K9 Committee, is based right here in Los Angeles. They sponsor dayhikes and weekend trips, led by volunteers, which specifically cater to people and their canine companions. One of the first organized canine hiking groups of its kind in the country, the K9 Committee conducts about a hundred hikes annually in the Los Angeles area, southern California and the west — almost all of them are free. To contact them, call the Angeles Chapter at (213)387-4287 or pick up a copy of the Angeles Chapter's Schedule of Activities, available at most outdoor equipment stores.

MAPS

At the beginning of each hike description in this book are the names of the maps for the area where the hiking trail is located. These maps are known as topographic maps (topos) which are surveyed and drawn by the United States Geographical Survey (USGS). Topos used to come in 15 minute (minute refers to latitude and longitude) quadrangles but are now available only in 7.5 minute quads since the former is being phased out by the USGS. Most of the maps are available at local outdoor equipment supply or travel stores. Many of the topos only show the geographical details of the land and not the trails, since most of the trails were constructed after the areas were surveyed and the maps printed.

Also available for the Santa Monica Mountains is a series of maps, which are highly recommended: "Trail Maps of the Santa Monica Mountains" by cartographer Tom Harrison. A set of these maps can be purchased from any outdoor equipment retailer in Southern California who sells maps, and at the National Park Headquarters at 30401 Agoura Road, #100 in Agoura Hills, just off the Ventura Freeway 101; phone: 818-597-9192. Free National Park Service maps are also available for some of the more popular recreation areas in the Santa Monica Mountains.

Directions to trailheads, driving instructions and recommendations for road maps are given at the beginning of each hike description. For most of the hikes listed in this book, the Automobile Club of Southern California Los Angeles and Vicinity map is recommended.

RATING THE HIKES

There are three classifications for each hike listed in this book — easy, moderate and strenuous, based on total mileage and elevation gain. There is no technical skill, such as those skills needed for rock-climbing with ropes, required of dog and owner for any of the hikes listed within the pages of this book.

It is recommended that both dogs and people be in good physical condition before embarking on any of the hikes. Dogs, like people, need to build up their strength and endurance for hiking. A dog can get just as tired and thirsty or be just as out-of-shape as a person. Every time you hike or walk, you help build up your physical endurance. Dogs and their owners can start getting into good condition by trying a few of the easy hikes listed in this book, then moving on to more difficult ones.

Generally, the hikes in the Santa Monica Mountains tend to be easier and closer to civilization. Hikes in the San Gabriel Mountains tend to more difficult and much farther away from civilization, which means that they are less traveled then their Santa Monica Mountain

Socializing canines on Vetter Mountain in the Angeles National Forest.

counterparts. If you and your dog are hiking alone for the first time, the author recommends trying Sulphur Springs Trail in Cheeseboro Canyon. It's a well-traveled trail which gently rambles through magnificent groves of oak and sycamore trees, staying essentially flat through the scenic countryside.

The difficulty rating for each route listed in this book is found at the beginning of each description. The ratings are as follows:

Easy: good hikes for dogs and people just starting out on the trail, older dogs, small dogs, out-of-shape dogs and people looking for some weekend exercise, or who are getting into shape for more challenging trips.

Moderate: dogs and people should be in good physical condition and have experience in doing several easy hikes.

Strenuous: dogs and people should be experienced hikers, in excellent physical condition, with some sort of daily exercise routine.

Ruins at Rocky Oaks.

2

The Santa Monica Mountains and Simi Hills

The canyons, ridges and grasslands of the Santa Monica Mountains are the perfect training ground for dogs and their human companions just beginning to hike together or intent on training for the more demanding terrain of the San Gabriel Mountains.

The Santa Monica Mountains create an impressive barrier along the Pacific Coast from Griffith Park in Los Angeles County on the east, to Point Mugu in Ventura County to the west; the Pacific Ocean to the south; the San Fernando and Conejo Valleys to the north; and the Los Angeles Basin to the southeast. This coastal range is rich in history. The Chumash, Fernandino and Gabrieleno people and their prehistoric ancestors were the first to live here. Spanish explorers and missionaries followed later, and by the end of the 19th century, pioneer families built their farms and worked their ranches in the mountains.

The plant communities of the Santa Monica Mountains are varied from coastal marsh along the ocean's tidewater zone to the coastal sage scrub and chaparral of the open, rolling ridges to the oak and riparian woodlands found in canyons and streambeds. Animals include a small population of mountain lions, mule deer, coyotes, rodents, and a variety of lizards, birds and snakes. The wildlife of the Santa Monica Mountains prefer to stay as far away from humans as possible. Yet, in some ways, one hopes not too far. There is something wonderful about hearing the yip of a coyote in the late afternoon as you and your dog walk along the peaceful ridgetops or through the grasslands of the Santa Monica Mountains.

The Simi Hills, Palo Comado and Cheeseboro Canyons are to the east of the Santa Monica Mountains. Their unique features include rugged sandstone cliffs, deep canyons, meandering streams, groves of sycamores and wide, open ridges, covered with oaks, grasses and an array of flora. The high point of the Simi Hills is Simi Peak (2,403'), which has nice views from the summit. It is a full day's hike from Cheeseboro Canyon via Palo Comado Canyon.

Trail to Sandstone Peak after 1993 firestorm.

WATER & SUN

The Santa Monica Mountains and Simi Hills get very hot during the summer months and it is recommended that plenty of water be carried during those times. Generally, the fall, winter and spring months are better suited for hiking the more demanding trails though there can be hot temperatures at any time during the year. Also, many of the trails are without the benefit of shade, particularly up on ridges. It is important to plan your hike accordingly.

FIRE

Over the years, devastating man-made fires have swept across the Santa Monica Mountains, killing wildlife and destroying vegetation. It takes years for the land to slowly come back to life.

During periods of great fire hazard, the National Park Service will post fire closures in areas of potential risk. However, when in doubt, call ahead.

Cheeseboro and Palo Comado Canyons

Cheeseboro Canyon became part of the Santa Monica Mountains National Recreation Area in the late 1980's and is under the jurisdiction of the National Park Service. The 2,308 acres of the old Jordan Ranch, which was purchased from comedian Bob Hope and added to the recreation area in 1994, includes beautiful Palo Comado, the large canyon to the west of Cheeseboro. To date, the purchase of Jordan Ranch represents the largest land acquisition in the Santa Monica Mountains National Recreation Area. A walk through Palo Comado is like walking through grazing lands of the old west. It was never developed, with the exception of a few jeep trails and corrals.

Cheeseboro Canyon has an extensive network of trails, ranging in difficulty from leisurely to strenuous. As of this writing, Palo Comado can be legally accessed on foot, by mountain bike or horse from the parking area at Cheeseboro Canyon though additional entrances to the canyon are planned. Few foot trails exist within the newly dedicated Palo Comado Canyon area. Most are old jeep trails.

The Park Service is still working on the funding to provide amenities like picnic tables, restrooms and trails. In fact, on one of our scouting trips to Palo Comado, we ran into two rangers on horseback who were in the process of exploring what appeared to be trails once used by the ranchers to herd sheep between Cheeseboro and Palo Commado. Palo Comado is truly an exceptional addition to the Santa Monica Mountains National Recreation Area. It is a wonderful place to explore and leashed dogs are welcome on all of the trails in both canyon areas.

We first walked the trails of Cheeseboro Canyon on a late spring weekend several years ago, before it was officially added to the national park system. The dirt parking lot was empty — there were no other people on the trails — just the sounds of crickets, the grasses rustling in the wind and the occasional cry of hawks circling in the sky.

That experience contrasted sharply with more recent trips to Cheeseboro Canyon following its addition to the park system. Though protected from urban development, the park is a very popular place on the weekends. The once quiet gem of the Santa Monica Mountains is now frequented by mountain bikers, equestrians, hikers, families and groups. Most of the visitors seem to stick to lower canyon trails, so it

Old caretaker's trailer for Jordan Ranch in Palo Comado Canyon is now gone.

is still possible to enjoy the tranquillity of the higher ridge trails, like the Baleen Wall Trail.

For the past 150 years, ranchers have grazed cattle in these hills and the effect of grazing on the land can be seen by the trained eye. Small arroyos, primarily created by over-grazing, are a land formation that did not exist prior to the introduction of cattle in the west and are evident in Palo Comado Canyon. Many of the native species of plants have been replaced by non-natives.

Both canyons are home to native species such as Coast Live Oak, Valley Oak, California Black Walnut, Willow, Lupine and Fuchsia-flowered Gooseberry. Non-native species like the exotic Tree Tobacco which is a native of South America, can be found in the uppermost regions of Palo Comado Canyon. An interesting note about the name Palo Comado. In Spanish, Palo means "thin trees" or "poles," yet there is no translation for "Comado." There has been some speculation that at one time the canyon was called "Palo Quemado" meaning "burned trees" in Spanish. As Anglo settlers moved into the area, it is believed that the Spanish name may have been spelled phonetically in English.

Cheeseboro and Palo Comado Canyons

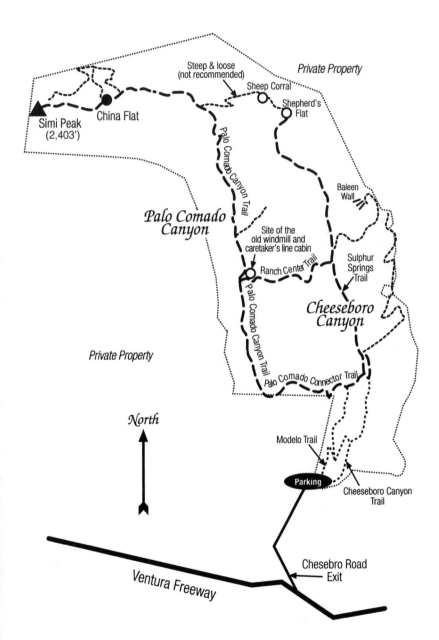

Steep & loose
(not recommended)

Sheep Corral

Shepherd's
Flat

Private Property

Simi Peak
(2,403')

China Flat

Palo Comado Canyon Trail

Baleen
Wall

*Palo Comado
Canyon*

Site of the
old windmill and
caretaker's line cabin

Ranch Center Trail

Sulphur
Springs
Trail

*Cheeseboro
Canyon*

Private Property

Palo Comado Canyon Trail

Palo Comado Connector Trail

North

Modelo Trail

Parking

Cheeseboro Canyon
Trail

Ventura Freeway

Chesebro Road
Exit

Tired baby. (Photo: Julie Rush)

Cheeseboro and Palo Comado Canyon Hikes

Classification: easy to strenuous as noted
K9 water: varies by hike — suggest minimum 1 quart for all hikes
Driving maps:
Automobile Club of Southern California: Los Angeles and Vicinity, Ventura County
Hiking maps:
USGS Calabasas 7.5 minute topo (most recent USGS update: 1967; does not show all trails in park), Thousand Oaks 7.5 minute topo
Best time to hike: upper ridge trails – November to April; canyon trails – all year, though water should be carried at all times, especially during the warm months of late spring and summer.

Driving:
From the Ventura Freeway 101, exit at Chesebro Road. Turn right on Palo Comado Road toward old Agoura Hills. Pass under "Old Agoura" sign and turn right at first stop sign, Chesebro Road.

Drive approximately 0.7 miles to the Cheeseboro Canyon Park entrance on the right (0.2 miles past a one lane bridge). Turn right into the park entrance and drive another 0.2 miles to a dirt parking area. There is a portable restroom in the parking area.

Note: all hikes for Cheeseboro/Palo Comado listed in this book start at the Cheeseboro parking lot described in the driving directions at the beginning of this section. As of this writing, the gate to the main parking lot opens at 8am and closes at sunset. If you think your hike might take you past sunset or you want to start a little earlier, park outside the park's entrance and walk in to the park.

Baleen Wall Trail, Cheeseboro Canyon

Classification: strenuous
K9 water: 2 quarts minimum on a moderate day
Well-conditioned dogs only
Posted: pets must be leashed
900' gain, 6.9 miles, 3 – 4 hours round-trip — strenuous

Hiking:
From the parking lot at Cheeseboro Canyon, walk straight ahead on the main dirt road, passing an informational sign. Paralleling the dirt road is a seasonal stream which meanders through the canyon, providing water to a variety of wildlife within the park. Once past the Overlook Trail sign on the right, the terrain opens up — grasslands, rounded open ridges and scattered oaks. About a half hour – forty-five minute walk from the parking lot, reach the Sulfur Springs/Baleen Wall Trails fork. Go right on the Baleen Wall Trail.

Follow the Baleen Wall Trail as it climbs out of the main canyon, up onto open ridges. The trail winds its way through the hills, passing a signed service road, a big water tank and some power lines. When the jagged, gray, teethy-looking Baleen Wall is in view and about 1/4 mile walk away (named after the Baleen Whale's teeth) notice a fork. The road to the right can be followed to the cliffs, where one can have a nice picnic lunch. To descend back into Cheeseboro Canyon, turn left at the same fork. The trail appears to head toward a lone powerline. About 200' past the fork, turn right onto a narrow foot path that quickly descends into Cheeseboro Canyon, but provides a nice view of the Baleen Wall on the way down. At the bottom of the canyon, turn left (west) and follow the trail through the canyon back to the parking lot.

Simi Peak (2,403') via Palo Comado Canyon

Classification: very strenuous
K9 water: 2 quarts minimum on a moderate day; no water on route
Well-conditioned dogs only
Posted: pets must be leashed
2,000' gain, 16 miles, 6 – 7 hours, round-trip on dirt road and jeep trail
Best time to hike: in moderate weather of late fall to spring, October –
late April There is little or no shade on most of the open ridges and
uphill segments of the hike. A few stands of oak are scattered along the
open ridges, but the canyons are well-shaded by old, stately oaks.

Hiking:
From the parking lot at Cheeseboro Canyon park entrance follow the
trail marked "Modelo Trail" on the left side of the parking lot. Walk the
trail as it climbs to an open ridge with a short, steep narrow canyon on
the right. At the top of the ridge, turn left at the fork, continuing on the
signed "Modelo Trail." The trail continues along the ridge top with
Cheeseboro Canyon to the right. Follow the trail over a slight rise and
down the other side to a second fork. Turn left at the second fork, the
Palo Comado Connector Trail (a right turn takes you back to Cheeseboro
Canyon and makes a nice easy, 3-mile loop). Follow the trail as it contours around a ridge, skirting several minor canyons. The trail finally
begins its descent into Palo Comado Canyon. The stables of a pony club
come into view at the canyon bottom. The trail passes to the right of the
stables. The trail (which is one of the old ranch jeep trails) meanders
through beautiful Palo Comado Canyon. When we scouted this hike, we
saw a herd of five mule deer just past the stables. There were also plenty of hawks and turkey buzzards flying in the sky above.

A little over a mile from the stables, you'll pass by some Southern
California Gas pipeline signs and come to a third, main trail fork. This
was the site of the last caretaker's dwelling (a dilapidated silver trailer)
for the old Jordan Ranch. When the first edition of this book came out,
the trailer and an old windmill were still standing at the fork and were
used as landmarks. Both have since been removed to prevent vandalism
and for liability reasons. The fork to the right, the Ranch Center Trail,
returns to Cheeseboro Canyon and will serve as the return route for this
hike. Continue north on the trail straight ahead to the left.

Follow the trail, as it leaves the canyon and begins a gradual, but steep ascent uphill. As the trail climbs steadily, jagged sandstone cliffs come into view. At the base of the first distinct set of cliffs is the old Sheep Corral Trail which was once used by the ranchers to herd sheep to and from neighboring Cheeseboro Canyon. Following the 1994 Northridge Earthquake and subsequent aftershocks, the trail was closed indefinitely due to landslides.

The main trail passes the cliffs and soon enters a vast, beautiful high valley, known as China Flats. Pass an old corral on the right and a road fork. Follow the left fork. A pond, used for watering livestock, comes into view on the left. About 1/4 mile past the corral, turn left at another fork and head towards the valley. At the next fork, stay right (the left fork goes down to Thousand Oaks). There is a small stream and rocky cliffs to the left of the trail. The trail leaves the valley, and comes to a saddle and another fork where Simi Valley comes into view. Continue straight ahead on the left fork. Follow the trail to the summit of Simi Peak. There is a fine view of Sandstone Peak, tallest mountain in the Santa Monicas to the west.

Return by the same route. When you reach the fork where the old caretaker's trailer used to be, turn left on the Ranch Center Trail. The trail climbs a steep ridge, but then quickly descends into Cheeseboro Canyon. At the bottom of the canyon, turn right and follow the trail back through the canyon to the parking lot. In the spring, following a good rain, the canyon is filled with the voices of hundreds of croaking frogs.

Palo Comado Canyon Trail to Cheeseboro Canyon via the Ranch Center Trail

Classification: moderate
K9 water: 2 quarts minimum on a moderate day;
no water on route
Posted: pets must be leashed
1,200' gain, 7.9 miles, 3 – 4 hours, round-trip on trail and dirt road
Best time to hike: October – late April

Hiking:

From the parking lot at Cheeseboro Canyon park entrance follow the trail marked "Modelo Trail" on the left side of the parking lot. Walk the trail as it climbs up an open ridge with a narrow canyon on the right. At the top of the ridge, turn left at the fork, continuing on the signed "Modelo Trail." The trail continues along the ridge top with Cheeseboro Canyon to the right. Follow the trail over a slight rise and down the other side to a second fork.

Turn left at the second fork. This is the Palo Comado Connector Trail (a right turn on this trail will take you back to the Sulphur Springs Trail in Cheeseboro Canyon). Follow the left fork, the trail contours around a ridge, skirting several minor canyons. The trail finally begins its descent into Palo Comado Canyon and the stables of a pony club become visible at the bottom. The trail passes to the right of the stables. The trail (which is one of the old ranch jeep trails) meanders through beautiful Palo Comado Canyon. When we scouted this hike, we saw a herd of five mule deer on the open ridges just past the stables. There were also plenty of hawks and turkey buzzards flying in the sky above.

A little over a mile from the stables, you'll pass by some Southern California Gas pipeline signs and come to a third, main trail fork. Just past the signs, was the old windmill, and the site of the last caretaker's dwelling on the old Jordan Ranch property. When this book was first written, both were still standing. Turn right at this fork (the left fork goes to Simi Peak), now named Ranch Center Trail. In the first edition of this book, we called this "The Old Windmill Hike," since the trail was not yet named, and there was a windmill at the fork. Follow the trail as it climbs a steep ridge. At the ridge crest, the trail steeply descends into Cheeseboro Canyon. At the bottom of the canyon, turn right and follow the trail back through the canyon to the parking lot.

The Modelo Trail to Cheeseboro Canyon

Classification: easy
K9 water: 1 quart minimum
Posted: pets must be leashed
550' gain, 2.9 miles hours, 2 hours round-trip on trail and dirt road
Best time to hike: October – late April

Hiking:
From the parking lot at Cheeseboro Canyon park entrance follow the trail marked "Modelo Trail" on the left side of the parking lot. Walk the trail as it climbs an open ridge with a narrow canyon on the right. At the top of the ridge, turn left at the fork, continuing on the signed "Modelo Trail." The trail continues along the ridge top with Cheeseboro Canyon to the right.

Follow the trail over a slight rise and down the other side to a second fork. Turn right at this fork, on the Palo Comado Connector Trail and follow the trail as it descends into Cheeseboro Canyon. At the canyon bottom, turn right, on the Sulphur Springs Trail, and follow it through Cheeseboro Canyon, back to the parking lot.

Sulphur Springs Trail, Cheeseboro Canyon

Classification: easy
K9 water: 1 quart minimum
Suitable for small or out-of-shape dogs
Posted: pets must be leashed
200' gain, 2.6 miles, 1–2 hours round-trip on trail and dirt road
Best time to hike: all year

Hiking:
From the parking lot at Cheeseboro Canyon, walk straight ahead on the main dirt road, passing an informational sign. Paralleling the dirt road is a seasonal stream which meanders through the canyon, providing water to a variety of wildlife within the park.

Follow the trail as it winds its way through the riparian habitat of the canyon. Once past the Overlook Trail sign on the right, the terrain opens up — grasslands, rounded open ridges and scattered oaks. About a half hour – forty-five minute walk from the parking lot, reach a fork and go left on the signed Sulphur Springs Trail (Baleen Wall Trail is on the right). Before 1997, this trail name was spelled both "Sulfur," and "Sulphur," on many of the same maps. The latter is now used by the Park Service on their new maps. Not far past the signed fork on the Sulphur Springs Trail, is a nice picnic area protected by the umbrella of oak branches and next to the little, rambling stream. Return by the same route.

Notes:
Any hike in Cheeseboro Canyon/Palo Comado can be sweltering during the summer, and very warm on any given day of the year. There is no shade on the high ridge trails and they are not recommended for hiking during the summer (unless done very early in the morning). The shorter hikes through the canyons are preferable during the summer months and suitable for the smallest of dogs. One of the most pleasant hikes in the valley on a warm summer evening is a walk to the picnic area on the Sulphur Springs Trail, about a half hour's walk from the main parking area. Cheeseboro Canyon is home to a diverse group of wildlife including several birds of prey. Golden eagles have been sighted in Palo Comado Canyon and around the Baleen Wall.

Evening light at Arroyo Sequit.

Arroyo Sequit

Classification: easy
K9 water: 1/2 quart; no water on route
Suitable for the smallest and most out-of-shape dogs
200' gain, 3/4 mile, 1 hour round-trip on paved and dirt road,
over grassy meadow
Posted: pets must be leashed
Driving maps:
Automobile Club of Southern California: Los Angeles and Vicinity
Hiking maps:
USGS Triunfo Pass 7.5 minute topo, Trail Map of the Santa Monica
Mountains, Central
Best time to hike: all year. Park gates open from 8am – 5pm.
Can be hot during summer.

Driving:
Exit Kanan Road from the Ventura Freeway 101 and go south on Kanan
Rd. At approximately 5.9 miles, turn right on Mulholland Highway. At
1.0 mile, continue right on Mulholland Hwy., at the Encinal Cyn.
Rd./Mulholland fork. At 3.2 miles make a left on CA – 23 south
(Westlake Blvd.). At 1.8 miles, turn right on Mulholland Hwy. Follow
Mulholland Hwy. approximately 1.7 miles to the entrance of Arroyo
Sequit on the left. Turn left into a small parking area, being careful not
to block the gated road.
Alternate driving route:
Exit Westlake Blvd., from the Ventura Fwy 101 and go south. Follow
Westlake Blvd. (Hwy 23 south) 6.9 miles to to Mulholland Highway and
turn right. Follow Mulholland approximately 1.7 miles to the entrance
of Arroyo Sequit on the left. Turn left into a small parking area, careful
not to block the gated road.

Hiking:
Walk past locked gate along the paved one-lane road, up a hill. At about
1/8 mile, turn left at a post marked "trail," bypassing the old farmhouse
residence on the right. The trail meets the road again, which is now dirt,
at a storage barn. There is a portable restroom and a circle of benches,
next to the old barn. Continue up the dirt road, and pass beneath large,

stately oaks (and one or two boisterous frogs) until you reach a large, open hilltop meadow with picnic tables located in various scenic places along the meadow. It's a wonderful place to have a picnic. To the north, you can see the massive, craggy peaks above Pt. Mugu.

The more adventurous types, can follow the dirt road to its end, just past a powerline. From the meadow, walk the dirt road south, staying right at a fork. The road narrows and drops down into a small canyon where occasionally quail can be sighted. Pass beneath a powerline and the road ends in a few hundred feet. Return by the same route.

Notes:

Arroyo Sequit was once an old pioneer ranch. Enjoy the peace and solitude of this little gem of the Santa Monicas. Arroyo Sequit is a great place to have a picnic or to celebrate a dog's birthday.

Paramount Ranch Hikes

Classification: easy to moderate as noted
K9 water: 1/2 quart to 2 quarts; no water on route
K9 and humans should not drink out of Medea Creek.
Posted: pets must be leashed
Driving maps:
Auto Club of Southern California: Los Angeles and Vicinity
Hiking Maps:
USGS Point Dume 7.5 minute topo Trail Map of the Santa Monica Mountains, Central

Driving:
Exit Kanan Road from the 101 Ventura Freeway and go south approximately 1/4 mile to signed Cornell Road. Turn left and follow Cornell Road approximately 1.8 miles to the signed park entrance on the right. Follow the main road, staying left, through an open area to a parking area and an information kiosk.

Paramount Ranch.

Walk of the Town

Classification: easy
K9 water: 1 quart; no water on route
Suitable for small or out-of-shape dogs
1/2 mile, 1/2-hour round-trip

Hiking:
From the parking area, pass the information kiosk and walk across a bridge, over Medea Creek, and follow signs to the western town. The town was used for several years as the setting for the television series "Dr. Quinn Medicine Woman," and scores of old western movies and television series. In fact, when we walked around the hills we found a script from the show laying on the trail. Walk around the town and then across the meadow to the old church and graveyard. Bring a blanket, a picnic lunch and sit awhile in the field.

Coyote Canyon Trail

Classification: easy
K9 water: 1 quart; no water on route
Suitable for small or out-of-shape dogs
100' gain, 3/4mile, 1/2 hour round-trip

Hiking:
Walk to the west side of town to the signed trail. Follow the narrow dirt trail as it meanders through a small canyon, paralleling a dry creek to the left of the trail. At approximately 1/8 mile, go right at a fork (fork is signed "Overlook Trail" which goes off to the left). The trail passes through an area of pink volcanic rock, as it contours along a grassy ridgeline. In another 1/8 mile, there is a picnic table on the left, about 100' off the trail and hidden in the chaparral. Continue along the trail until it returns to the paved road behind the town and a large grove of eucalyptus trees. Turn right and follow the paved road back to town.

Medea Creek Trail (aka Stream Terrace Trail)

Classification: easy
K9 water: 1 quart
K9s and humans should not drink from Medea Creek.
Suitable for small or out-of-shape dogs
300' gain, 1 mile, 3/4 hour round-trip

Hiking:
From the information kiosk, walk south across the parking lot past a gated road on the right. On the right, about 100 feet past the gated road is the signed Medea Creek Trail. Follow this narrow use trail as it gradually climbs uphill through thick chaparral and oaks, paralleling the road for about 100 feet or so. Follow the trail as it contours the densely vegetated ridge by a series of short switchbacks, out to an open area and the highway. Turn right at the "5K Trail" fork just before the highway. Continue on the trail to the next fork. If you go right at the fork, you can climb a small hill, via a return loop trail, to a vista point which overlooks the Paramount Ranch and Medea Creek. Return to the main trail, via the loop, and descend gradually back into the canyon. As you descend, the prominent peak across the wash is named Sugarloaf Peak. At the canyon bottom, turn right and follow the dirt road back to the locked gate and parking lot. Medea Creek parallels the dirt road on the left.

Rocky Oaks Hikes (see photo on page 36)

Classification: easy
Posted: pets must be leashed
K9 water: 1/2 – 1 quart; no water on route
Rocky Oaks Loop Trail & Rocky Oaks Creek Trail: suitable for small or out-of-shape dogs
Driving maps:
Auto Club of Southern California: Los Angeles and Vicinity
Hiking maps:
USGS Point Dume 7.5 minute topo, Trail Map of the Santa Monica Mountains, Central
Best time to hike: all year. These trails, like most in the Santa Monica Mountains, can be very hot during late spring, summer and early fall — be sure to carry more water at those times. Rocky Oaks is very popular with equestrians from neighboring ranches and camps.

Driving:
Exit Kanan Road from the Ventura Freeway 101 and go south to Mulholland Highway. Turn right on Mulholland and at 0.1 mile turn right again into park entrance. There is ample parking in the dirt parking lot. Both hikes start from same point near the information kiosk in the parking lot.

Hiking:
Rocky Oaks Loop Trail
200' gain, 1.5 miles, 1 hour round-trip
From the information kiosk at the west end of parking lot (near the entrance) follow the main trail north to a signed trail fork — "Rocky Oaks Loop Trail – Creek Trail." Turn left at a sign and follow the trail as it curves to the right, passing old ranch ruins and antique farming equipment on the left. At approximately 1/8 mile from the sign, you come to a three-way fork, with the signed Creek Trail on the left. Continue straight on the Loop Trail, heading uphill passing through some wood posts, eventually contouring around a south facing slope (no shade). The trail contours around the ridge passing a small use trail on the left. About 25' from the main trail on this use trail, there is a sign marking the "Overlook Trail" on the left. For a nice 360-degree view of

Rocky Oaks, follow the "Overlook Trail" to the left, to a small open area about 100' from the Loop Trail. Return to the loop trail by the same route.

After returning to the main trail, continue contouring around the ridge toward Kanan Road. At a fork just before the highway (which is separated from the park by a fence), turn right and descend into a canyon of meadows and oaks. At the next fork (signed Pond Trail) continue left on the Loop Trail. Go right at the next fork (signed Glade Trail) following the trail through a meadow, where crickets can often be heard chirping. At a four-way fork, continue straight ahead, following the sign to the parking lot. Stay left at the next fork and pass through a pleasant shaded picnic area, just before the parking lot. There is a water fountain in the picnic area and restrooms at the parking lot.

Rocky Oaks Creek Trail

Minimal gain; 1 mile round-trip, 45 minutes round-trip
From the information kiosk at the west end of the parking lot (near the entrance), follow the main trail north to a signed trail fork — "Rocky Oaks Loop Trail – Creek Trail." Turn left at the sign and follow the trail as it curves to the right, passing old ranch ruins and antique farming equipment on the left. Approximately 1/8 mile from the sign, you come to a three-way fork, with the signed Creek Trail on left. Turn left and walk across the field to a narrow use trail which parallels a dry creek. Follow the trail about a quarter mile through oaks and scrub, before the park boundary. Return by the same route.

Notes:
The Rocky Oaks area, with its year-round spring, was once home to various bands of coastal Chumash Indians, but any traces of their existence were destroyed by subsequent years of farming and ranching. At the turn of the century, the Thompson family built their ranch above the spring, and raised crops and a few head of cattle. Life was not easy in the Santa Monica Mountains and the family endured the hardships of nature, experiencing fires, floods, windstorms and drought. In 1950, the Brown family built their farm here, naming it "Rocky Oaks", raising cattle and crops. In 1980, they sold the property to the Park Service. The Agoura fire of 1978 destroyed all traces of the Thompson's early pioneer ranch. There is a nice, shaded picnic area located on the east side of the parking lot.

Peter Strauss Ranch (Lake Enchanto)

This is another site in the Santa Monica Mountains which was once inhabited by the Chumash people, but where any trace of their existence has all but disappeared. Only the trained archaeologist would be able to locate any evidence of their habitation. In 1923, a man name Harry Miller, built the stone ranch house, caretaker's quarters, aviary and other stone structures still standing on the site today.

During the late 1930's, millionaire Charles Hinman purchased the property and constructed a small dam on Triunfo Creek. The lake, created by the dam, was named Lake Enchanto. In 1939, a swimming pool, the largest pool on the West Coast at the time, was built to the west of the main ranch house. Around the 1950's, Lake Enchanto became a popular amusement park and children's summer camp. In the 1970's, Hinman lost the property in a tax sale, and Lake Enchanto fell into disuse. As a kid, I remember driving by the old, decrepit place with my parents on a weekend excursion to the beach in the sixties and wondering what was going on behind the strange stone tower and entrance.

In 1977, actor Peter Strauss purchased the property which was covered with the rusted ruins of Lake Enchanto's abandoned amusement rides. He lived at the ranch house from 1977 to 1983, where he spent hundreds of thousands of dollars on the removal of all the abandoned structures and debris left over from Lake Enchanto days, landscaping and general improvements on the property. Peter Strauss later sold the ranch to the Santa Monica Mountains Conservancy. In 1987, the National Park Service purchased it from the Conservancy.

The cactus garden at Lake Enchanto.

Peter Strauss Trail

Classification: easy
K9 water: 1/2 quart
Suitable for small or out-of-shape dogs
Peter Strauss Trail: 200' gain, 0.6 mile, 1/2 hour round-trip
Posted: pets must be leashed
Driving maps:
Auto Club of Southern California: Los Angeles and Vicinity
Hiking maps:
USGS Point Dume 7.5 minute topo, Trail Map of the Santa Monica
Mountains, Central
Best time of year to hike: all year. Late winter and spring are the best
times to catch wildflowers in bloom. Open daily from 8am to 5pm.

Driving:
Exit Kanan Road from the Ventura Freeway 101 and head south approximately 2.8 miles to Troutdale Drive. Turn left and follow Troutdale
about 0.4 mile to Mulholland Highway. Turn left at Mulholland, cross
over a bridge and turn right into a parking area.

Hiking:
From the parking area, follow a foot path back across the bridge and left
into the gated Peter Strauss Ranch. Straight ahead is the beautiful old
stone ranch house, built in 1923, along with the caretaker's place on the
hill behind the house, and the aviary (which is empty today). There are
restrooms on the west side of the ranch house.

Pass the east side of the ranch house and aviary to the signed Peter
Strauss Trail. Follow the trail to a signed fork (Peter Strauss Trail)—
go right at the fork. The trail switchbacks along a densely wooded
slope. Stay left at the next fork, on a maintained trail. Herds of mule
deer are often seen in the woodlands along the trail. After contouring
the shaded ridge for some time, the trail begins to descend down terraced stone steps, through lush fern growth, back to the main trail. Turn
left at the main trail, back towards the main ranch house. The trail parallels the ephemeral Triunfo Creek to the right.

Sandstone Peak (3,111'), Circle X Ranch

Classification: moderate
K9 water: 1/2 quart – 1 quart; no water on route
Suitable for small, well-conditioned dogs
2.2 miles, 1,000' elevation gain, 2 hours round-trip
Posted: pets must be leashed
Driving maps:
Auto Club of Southern California: Los Angeles and Vicinity
Hiking maps:
USGS Triunfo Pass 7.5 minute topo, Trail Map of the Santa Monica Mountains, West
Best time of year to hike: all year though summers can be sweltering. Late winter and spring are the best times to catch wildflowers in bloom. Open daily from 8am to sunset.

Driving:
From the Ventura Freeway 101 exit Westlake Blvd – California 23 South. Drive south on Westlake Blvd./CA 23 South 6.9 miles to Mulholland Highway. Turn right on Mulholland and at 0.3 miles, turn right again on Little Sycamore Canyon Road. Continue on Little Sycamore (which becomes Yerba Buena Road) for 4.3 miles to the Backbone Trail parking lot on the right.

Hiking:
From the north end of the parking lot, walk past the information kiosk and locked gate to the Backbone Trail. Follow the trail as it climbs steadily through what is usually dense coastal chaparral and shrub. However, at the time of this writing, the chaparral and scrub are gone, replaced by the thousands of acres of open, charred terrain created by the firestorm of 1993. Despite the fact that everything burned here, there is still a certain, unusual beauty to the terrain, that everyone should experience.

Just follow the trail as it switchbacks a few times up to an open, flat area, where the trail is partially paved. To the left (southeast) are steps leading to the summit of Sandstone Peak and a sign which points the way. Walk the steps to a small use trail which traverses over pink volcanic rock, requiring some scrambling, to the summit, which is marked

On the trail to the summit of Sandstone.

by a summit register and a monument to W. Herbert Allen. Allen was a major supporter of the Circle X Ranch, which was initially created as a camp for children in the late 1940's.

Notes:
On a clear day, the 360 degree view from the summit of Sandstone Peak is spectacular! Looking southeast across the Pacific Ocean, one can see Santa Catalina, San Clemente, Santa Barbara and San Nicholas islands; to the west — the Channel Islands: Anacapa, Santa Cruz, Santa Rosa and San Miguel. To the north, the peaks of the Los Padres National Forest; to the east, Mt. Baldy in the San Gabriel Mountains and sometimes even San Gorgonio Peak in the San Bernadino Mountains.

Latigo Canyon to Castro Crest
via the Backbone Trail

Classification: easy – moderate
K9 water: minimum 1 quart; no water on route
Suitable for small, conditioned dogs
1,030' gain, 4.4 miles, 2 1/2 hours round-trip on trail and fire road
Driving maps:
Auto Club of Southern California: Los Angeles and Vicinity,
Ventura County
Hiking maps:
USGS Point Dume 7.5 minute topo; Santa Monica Mountains Trail
Guide
Best time to hike: all year, though during the summer months, the hike,
which is without shade until the crest is reached, can be extremely hot.

Driving:
From the Ventura Freeway 101, exit Kanan Road and drive south (toward
the Pacific Ocean) approximately 6.4 miles to Latigo Canyon Road and
turn left. Drive another 2.9 miles to the signed "Backbone Trail" parking area on the left.

Hiking:
From the parking area, walk north on the signed "Backbone Trail."
Follow the trail up a short rise and then down into the lush, fern-covered
upper part of Newton Canyon drainage. The trails drops into the canyon
bottom and crosses over ephemeral Newton Creek. On the other side of
the creek, the trail begins to climb up the east side of the canyon, eventually leaving the canyon. Follow the trail as it contours along the southern slopes of Castro Peak (identified by the all of the radio antennae on
the summit) to a saddle, approximately 1.4 miles from the parking area.

At the signed saddle, turn left toward Castro Peak. Hike another 0.8
miles to a second saddle which is covered by oaks, and where three trails
forks converge. This is the end of the hike and lunch can be enjoyed
beneath the oaks or on top of a small flat area to the south. The two trails
to the left, go within a 0.2 mile of the summit of Castro Peak. The third
fork, to the right, can be followed about fifty feet to a flat area, on the
ridge with great views to the Pacific. The summit of Castro Peak, which

is owned by the County of Los Angeles, is closed to hikers, however the view of the San Fernando Valley and San Gabriel Mountains is quite nice. Return to the parking area by the same route.

A pleasant-looking National Park man checked me in
and then he said, "How about that dog?
They aren't permitted in except on leash."
"Why?" I asked.
"Because of the bears."
"Sir," I said, "this is an unique dog. He does not live by
tooth or fang. He respects the rights of cats to be cats although he
doesn't admire them. He turns his steps rather than disturb
an earnest caterpillar. His greatest fear is that someone will point
out a rabbit and suggest he chase it.
This is a dog of peace and tranquility. I suggest that the greatest
danger to your bears will be pique at being ignored by Charley."

John Steinbeck, *Travels with Charley* • 1961

The Mueller Tunnel on the trail to Mt. Lowe from Eaton Saddle.

3

The San Gabriel Mountains

The San Gabriel Mountains are an impressive range, where on any given summer's day, large, magnificent thunderheads gather above the crest in the late afternoon. The range creates a rugged five to ten thousand foot wall of steep ridges and boulder-filled canyons between the Los Angeles basin and the Mojave Desert.

Throughout history, people have been drawn for various reasons to the San Gabriel Mountains. The earliest visitors to the San Gabriels were the Native Americans — Gabrielino, Serrano and Fernandinos — who drank from the mountain streams, hunted deer, and gathered pine nuts and acorns from groves of pinyon pine and oak trees. Later, Spaniards explored routes across the passes, and miners prospected for gold and other minerals. Ranchers fought for the rights to the water that cascaded down the canyons. Pioneers and others who crossed this continent to find their fortunes in the west, cut the timber and collected streambed rocks to build their homes.

The San Gabriel Mountains are also home to a diverse collection of shrubs and trees called chaparral which include yucca, wild lilac, mountain mahogany, laurel and manzanita. Forests of pine — Jeffrey, Ponderosa, Coulter, and Lodgepole, Incense Cedar and White Fir — can be found above the chaparral at higher elevations.

There are also mule deer, a small population of black bears and mountain lions, and bighorn sheep in addition to smaller animals like chipmunks, squirrels, skunks, raccoons, bobcats and weasels. Due to human encroachment into the mountains, the larger animals tend to avoid contact with people and generally pose no danger to humans unless cornered or threatened.

When you visit the San Gabriel Mountains, to fully enjoy the experience, you should always be prepared. Though the mountains are easily reached from Los Angeles by car, trails are often a fair distance from a telephone or ranger's office. Carry the right equipment, including water, food and proper clothing. The weather can change at any time, from sunshine one moment, to the thunder and lightning of a sudden storm the next. If you're walking the mountain trails, avoid cutting switchbacks (short-cutting) which erode the trail both physically and visually. Leave the radios at home, so you can listen to the sound of the wind whispering through the pines. Be courteous to others you meet along the trail who, like you, are also wishing to share in the unique mountain experience. "Take only pictures. Leave only footprints."

To park in the National Forests in southern California, a daily "Adventure Pass" must be purchased prior to entry. The United States Forest Service sells the "Adventure Passes," recreation maps, and provides a number of free informational pamphlets about the Angeles Forest and San Gabriel Mountains. The maps show the trails, dirt roads, campgrounds, landmarks and other points of interest. The "Adventure Pass" may also be purchased from sporting good stores and some local shops or gas stations near entry points to the forests. It's purpose is to help defray USFS operational costs. Maps, passes and additional information can be obtained from the USFS at:

Angeles National Forest Headquarters
701 N. Santa Anita
Arcadia, CA 91006
(818) 574-5200

Arroyo Seco District
Oak Grove Park
Flintridge, CA 91011
(818) 790-1151

Tujunga District
12371 N. Little Tujunga Canyon Road
San Fernando, CA 91342
(818)889-1900

Mt. Baldy District
110 N. Wabash
Glendora, CA 91740
(818)335-1251

Haines Canyon flood control along streambed after a wet year. 71

Haines Canyon Streamside Walk

Classification: easy
K9 water: 1 quart; water in stream on route
Suitable for small dogs.
300' gain, 2 miles, 1-1.5 hours round-trip on fire road and trail
Driving map:
Auto Club of Southern California: Los Angeles and Vicinity
Hiking maps:
USGS Sunland and Condor Peak 7.5 minute topos
Best time to hike: year-round, can be very warm during the summer.
Watch for poison oak on the use-trail return route.

Driving:
Take I-210 to the Lowell Avenue offramp. Exit and follow Lowell north
past Foothill Blvd to Day Street. Turn left (west) on Day Street and follow to Haines Canyon Avenue. Turn right (north) on Haines Canyon.
Go two blocks to end of road and park, careful not to block entrances of
private residences.

Hiking:
Walk up Haines Canyon, which turns to dirt at the end of the pavement,
passing private residences and the fenced Haines Canyon Debris Basin
on the right. During the flood of 1969, this debris basin, like so many
others in the San Gabriels, filled up with rocks and debris that washed
down the canyons. The basin filled up so quickly, that the City of Los
Angeles wasn't able to empty it fast enough, and consequently, it over-
topped.

Walk past a locked gate and follow the main fire road, staying right
at the first two forks within first 1/4 mile. The drainage on the right, parallels the road all the way up the canyon. At about 3/4 mile, pass a grove
of sycamore trees and the ruins of a cabin on a terrace above the trees.
Although not visible from the road, the ruins are accesible from the road
by a small footpath. Continue on the fireroad, until you reach a large
boulder strewn wash that crosses the road. Sometimes water is flowing
across the road here. Turn right at the fork just on the other side of the
wash and walk past an unlocked gate. About twenty feet past the gate
and to the right, is a well-worn use trail that drops down into the lush

Haines Canyon Debris Basin.

fern-covered drainage of Haines Canyon. Watch for posion oak along the way. Follow the trail back to the small plateau just above the debris basin pond, careful not to wander off onto one of the many forks to the left which will take you into the next drainage to the east. When you reach the plateau, walk back to the fireroad and follow it back down to Haines Canyon Avenue.

Notes:
There are some old cabin ruins with great fireplaces made of stream bed stones in the wash, victims of the great flood of 1938 and subsequent fires. Purple vinca and English ivy are all that's left of the gardens planted by the early canyon settlers. In the spring, locals pick the stinging nettles in the canyon for cooking in exotic dishes from their homeland. You might meet them along the way carrying bags full of freshly picked nettles, however, we definitely suggest that you don't pick the nettles or any other plant in the area (and certainly don't eat them)! Stinging nettles are mighty unpleasant if touched by people or dogs and cause a long-lasting, burning rash. The fire road and trail are also used by equestrians from the local area.

Mt. Lukens (5,074') from Haines Canyon

Classification: strenuous
K9 water: 2 quarts minimum; water in stream at beginning of hike in canyon
Well-conditioned, experienced dogs only.
Posted: pets must be leashed
3,000' gain, 9 miles, 6-7 hours round-trip on fire road
Driving map:
Auto Club of Southern California: Los Angeles and Vicinity
Hiking map:
USGS Condor Peak and Sunland 7.5 minute topos
Best time to hike: October to May.
Trail can be extremely hot during the summer and there is no shade above the canyon.

Driving:
Take I-210 to the Lowell Avenue offramp. Exit and follow Lowell north past Foothill Blvd to Day Street. Turn left (west) on Day Street and follow to Haines Canyon Avenue. Turn right (north) on Haines Canyon. Go two blocks to end of road and park, careful not to block entrances of private residences.

Hiking:
Walk up Haines Canyon, which turns to dirt at the end of the pavement, passing private residences and the fenced Haines Canyon Debris Basin on the right. During the flood of 1969, this debris basin like so many others in the San Gabriels, over-topped.

Walk past a locked gate and follow the main fire road to the right of the first fork. The drainage on the right, parallels the road all the way up the canyon. Follow the dirt road as it climbs steadily up the canyon to the summit of the peak. There is no shade once you leave the canyon.

There are a number of electronic installations on the summit, however, these do not interfere with the spectacular view of the Big Tujunga watershed, and (on a clear day) all the way across the Los Angeles basin out to the Pacific Ocean. Mt. Lukens is very popular with mountain bikers who ride up from Angeles Crest Highway to the east.

Author with Tama. (PHOTO: Terry Austin)

Notes:
The hike to Mt. Lukens from Haines Canyon admidst the fragrant aromas of the chaparral, up the old JPL fire road, is a good, scenic workout, for canines and their human compatriots preparing for more significant endeavors. In the canyon are a number of old cabin sites, the stone foundations of which are covered with English ivy, purple vinca and native flora. One of the most interesting of these sites is perched on a hillside above a grove of sycamores, only about a mile up the canyon. During the summer, the dirt road can be very hot and dusty, so an early morning start is recommended.

Mt. Lukens is the highest mountain within Los Angeles City limits. The peak was originally named by the U.S. Army's Wheeler Survey topographers "Sister Elsie Peak" after a Catholic nun who ran an orphanage for Native American children. In the twenties, the USFS renamed the peak after Theodore P. Lukens, mayor of Pasadena in 1894, noted for his efforts in reforestation. The fire lookout, which was built on the summit by the USFS in 1927, was moved to Josephine Peak in 1937.

Gould Mesa to Arroyo Seco

Classification: easy
K9 water: 1/2 quart; water in stream on route
Suitable for small dogs or out-of-shape dogs
Posted: pets must be leashed
700' gain, 4.5 miles, 2 hours round-trip on dirt road
Driving map:
Auto Club of Southern California: Los Angeles and Vicinity
Hiking maps:
USGS Arroyo Seco 7.5 minute topo
Best time to hike: all year, except during periods of heavy rains or high water.

Driving:
Take I-210 to Angeles Crest Highway (2) in La Canada and exit. Drive north on Angeles Crest Highway approximately 2 miles to a dirt parking area on the right side of the road, just above the La Canada-Flintridge Country Club.

Hiking:
Park and walk a few feet to the driveway just above the parking area. Follow the paved driveway past a locked gate passing the humming Gould Substation on your right (named after 19th century Arroyo homesteader, Will Gould). The paved road climbs a short, steep hill, then quickly descends into the canyon of the Arroyo Seco. The road soon turns to dirt after passing beneath a stately oak tree.

About 1.3 miles from Angeles Crest Highway, the dirt road reaches the bottom of the canyon, the old Arroyo Seco Road, the USFS Angeles National Forest boundary and Gould Mesa Campground (there is a restroom) — a favorite camp with mountain bikers.

At Gould Mesa, the road forks. To the left, the historic dirt road continues up the Arroyo Seco to Paul Little Picnic Area (0.7 miles, one-way), the Oak Wilde Campground (3.2 miles one-way), eventually reaching Switzer's Camp and Eaton Saddle.

For this hike, turn right and follow the road as it meanders through the canyon, paralleling the creek. Note an old gauging station and the ruins of cabins on either side of the creek. Follow the dirt road, past several bridges to the southern boundary of the Angeles National Forest. Return by the same route.

Notes:
This is a wonderful conditioning hike for dogs readying for more difficult conquests. With the exception of the first mile, the hike is fairly flat. There are numerous stream crossings which can be fairly deep during the winter months and impassable during heavy rains. In fact, it is a good idea to stay out of the San Gabriel Mountain canyons during rain storms, since the canyons serve as drainage for many square miles of mountain terrain above them, and are prone to heavy run-off at these times. .

Gould Mesa to Oak Wilde

Classification: moderate
K9 water: 1/2 quart; water in stream on route
Suitable for small, well-conditioned dogs
Posted: pets must be leashed
1,300' gain, 9 miles, 4.5 hours round-trip on dirt road, narrow trail with at least 15 stream crossings
Driving map:
Auto Club of Southern California: Los Angeles and Vicinity
Hiking map:
USGS Arroyo Seco 7.5 minute topo
Best time to hike: all year, except during periods of heavy rains or high water.

Driving:
Take I-210 to Angeles Crest Highway-2 in La Canada and exit. Drive north on Angeles Crest Highway approximately 2 miles to a dirt parking area on the right side of the road, just above the La Canada-Flintridge Country Club.

Hiking:
Park and walk a few feet to the driveway just above the parking area. Follow the paved driveway past a locked gate passing the humming Gould Substation (named after 19th century Arroyo homesteader, Will Gould). The paved road climbs a short, steep hill, then quickly descends into the canyon of the Arroyo Seco. The road soon turns to dirt after passing beneath a stately oak tree.

About 1.3 miles from Angeles Crest Highway, the dirt road reaches the bottom of the canyon, the old Arroyo Seco Road, the USFS Angeles National Forest boundary and Gould Mesa Campground (there is a restroom) — a favorite camp with mountain bikers. At Gould Mesa, the road forks. To the left, the historic dirt road continues up the Arroyo Seco to Paul Little Picnic Area (.7 miles, one-way), the Oak Wilde Campground (3.2 miles one-way), eventually reaching Switzer's Camp and beyond that, Eaton Saddle.

Cooling off for just a moment in the upper Arroyo.

For this hike, turn left up the canyon, paralleling the creek to your right. Along the trail are the stone foundations of mountain cabins built around the turn of the century. Many of these stone ruins can be spotted amidst groves of decades-old cactus and century plants. English Ivy, purple vinca and paper whites are all that's left of the gardens planted by the canyon dwellers before the great flood of 1938. About fifteen minutes from Gould Mesa campground, you'll pass Niño Campground on the left. Approximately 1.7 miles (and about 9 boot-soaking stream crossings) from the Gould Mesa Campground, you'll reach Paul Little Picnic Area. At the picnic area, the trail forks. To the right, is the Gabrielino Trail which continues on to Oak Wilde. To the left is the picnic area, a pit restroom and a use trail which leads to the base of the Brown Canyon Debris Basin. Stop and rest at one of the tables set on terraced slopes over-looking the Arroyo.

Continue from the picnic area on the trail fork to the right, which climbs and traverses a steep ridge before dropping back into the arroyo. From this trail, look down upon the Brown Canyon Debris Basin. Once back in the canyon, follow the trail as it zigzags back and forth, across a sandy wash (and many more stream crossings), finally reaching OakWilde campground. Relax and enjoy the sounds of the canyon from one of the many picnic tables. Notice a huge oleander and an old lemon tree — all that remains of the garden plantings from the early days. Return to Gould Mesa by the same route.

Notes:

As early as 1884, there was a mountain resort established high in the canyon known as Switzer's Camp, and by 1911 a tourist camp was built at what is now Oak Wilde Campground. Since the late 1800's, thousands of visitors traveled this dirt road up the canyon. Some of the famous visitors who signed the guest register at Switzer's included Clark Gable, Mary Pickford, Henry Ford, Joan Crawford and Shirley Temple. By 1935, the USFS recorded at least 127 privately-owned cabins (on leased USFS land) in the lower Arroyo Seco Canyon.

The "Great Flood of 1938" and subsequent floods since then, washed away many of the cabins, the old road, and changed the course of the stream on more than one occasion. Evidence of this is the Elmer Smith bridge (south of Gould Mesa Campground) which, at the time of this writing, was suspended over a dry channel with a "no fishing from bridge" sign hanging from the bridge. "Arroyo Seco" was the Spanish name for "dry brook" which perhaps, is a more accurate description for the section of the Arroyo below Devil's Gate Reservoir.

Mt. Lowe (5,603') from Eaton Saddle

Classification: easy – moderate
K9 water: 1 quart; no water on route
Suitable for small, well-conditioned dogs.
500' gain, 3 miles, 2 hours round-trip on dirt road and trail
Driving map:
Auto Club of Southern California: Los Angeles and Vicinity
Hiking map:
USGS Mount Wilson 7.5 minute topo
Best time to hike: all year, though most enjoyable weather (as is true for most of the lower peaks in the San Gabriel Mountains) can be found during the months of April to November.

The Mt. Wilson road is open year-round, though sometimes during winter, the road is occasionally closed because of snow or rock slides. Recommend leashing dogs from parking area at Eaton Saddle until you reach the Mueller Tunnel due to steep cliffs along that portion of the trail.

Driving:
Take I-210 to Angeles Crest Highway (2) in La Canada and exit. Drive north on Angeles Crest Highway approximately 14 miles to Red Box. Turn right here on the Mt. Wilson Road and drive 2.3 miles to Eaton Saddle. Park in a large dirt parking area, careful not to block the locked gate.

Hiking:
Walk past the locked gate and follow the dirt road, passing sheer drop-offs to your left and steep walls to your right. Pass through the Mueller Tunnel, named for A. J. "Hap" Mueller, who beginning in 1925, was charged with building an elaborate network of firebreaks and fire roads for the United States Forest Service in the San Gabriel Mountains. Just before you enter the tunnel, look at the cliffs just to the left and slightly above the tunnel. There are some old railings clinging to the rocky precipice, stoic reminders of the original hair-raising trail to Mt. Lowe before the road and tunnel were built by the Forest Service. Continue on to Markham Saddle. At Markham Saddle the road starts to head down-hill, off to the right. Leave the road at the saddle by turning left onto a foot path (USFS trail 12W14), which quickly rises above the road, paralleling it for some time, through oaks and chaparral. Follow this pleasant

trail to a saddle between Mt. Markham and Mt. Lowe. Continue south past the saddle approximately 200 yards to a junction. Turn right (west) on the trail which will take you to the summit of Mt. Lowe.

Notes:

The history of Mt. Lowe is certainly one of the most colorful of all the peaks in the San Gabriel Mountains. In 1891, funded by Professor Thaddeus Lowe from Pasadena, construction began on the Mt. Lowe Railway. At that time, it was considered to be one of the engineering wonders of the world. Collaborating with engineer David Joseph Macpherson, who located the rail route, Lowe built the first electrically-powered incline mountain railway in the world.

In 1892, while the railway was under construction, Lowe escorted, on horseback, a group of VIPs from Pasadena on a tour of the area. The trip ended on what was then known as Oak Mountain. As the group stood on the summit of the peak, someone proposed renaming the peak Mt. Lowe, in honor of their guide and host. Everyone present thought it was a great idea, and so Mt. Lowe came to be.

From 1893 to 1935, during the peak years of operation for the Mt. Lowe Railway, thousands of people rode the railway from Mountain Junction in Altadena, 1,300'to Echo Mountain. There they found a hotel, a casino-dance hall, a zoo, an observatory, several residences, a power plant and the "Great Searchlight," which was then, the world's largest searchlight. In 1895, "Ye Alpine Tavern" was formally opened 1,000' below the summit of Mt. Lowe. From the tavern, visitors could ride the guided "pony train" or hike on two-well maintained trails to the summit of Mt. Lowe. Unfortunately, beginning as early as 1900, a series of disastrous fires, subsequent floods and other ill-fated events, all but eradicated any trace of the mountain's glorious past.

The trail from Eaton Saddle to Mt. Lowe tends to be hot and dusty during the summer months, but oak trees along the trail and near the summit provide some shade. The trail to Mt. Lowe is very popular and well-traveled. On a clear day, there are great views of the Los Angeles basin, out to the Pacific ocean and Catalina Island.

Josephine Peak (5,558')

Classification: moderate
K9 water: 1 - 1.5 quarts; no water on route
A rigorous challenge for small, well-conditioned dogs.
1,900' gain, 8 miles, 5.5 hours round-trip on dirt road
Driving map:
Auto Club of Southern California: Los Angeles and Vicinity
Hiking map:
USGS Condor Peak 7.5 minute topo
Best time to hike: late September to early May.
On rare occasion during the winter months, there can be some snow
on Mt. Josephine. Can be very hot during summer.

Driving:
Take I-210 to Angeles Crest Highway (2) in La Canada and exit. Drive
north on Angeles Crest Highway approximately 9.5 miles to the Angeles
Forest Highway (N3). Turn left and park in the dirt parking area on the
west side of Angeles Forest Highway.

Hiking:
Cross the highway to a dirt road on the west side of Angeles Forest
Highway. Follow the dirt road as it meanders up some swithcbacks, two
miles to a junction. From this junction, you have a beautiful view to the
east of Strawberry Peak, across Josephine Saddle. To the west, is the
route to Josephine Peak. Continue to the left (west) up the fire road, to
the summit of Josephine Peak. The ruins of the old fire lookout, in the
form of a concrete foundation, mark the summit.

Notes:
Josephine Peak is best hiked during mild weather, since there is no
shade along the road, with the exception of a few pine trees near the
summit. In 1937, a fire lookout was constructed on the summit and
remained in service until it burned down in 1976. Josephine Peak was
named after Josephine Lippencott, who was married to USGS surveyor
Joseph Barlow Lippencott, who used Josephine Peak for a survey station in 1894.

Strawberry Peak (6,164')

Classification: moderate – strenuous
K9 water: 1.5 – 2 quarts; no water on route
1,500' gain, 6 miles, 5 – 6 hours round-trip
Driving map:
Auto Club of Southern California: Los Angeles and Vicinity
Hiking maps:
USGS Condor Peak and Chilao Flat 7.5 minute topos
Best time to hike: October to May.
Strawberry Peak can be hiked during the summer, but tends to get very hot along the trail. During the winter months, the trail can be very icy when snow is present.

Driving:
Take I-210 to Angeles Crest Highway (2) in La Canada and exit. Drive north on Angeles Crest Highway approximately 14 miles to Red Box. Park in paved parking area just off the Angeles Crest Highway.

Hiking:
From the parking area, cross the highway and walk east approximately 100' to a dirt road on the left (2N46). Walk the dirt road as it parallels the highway for about 3/4 mile to a junction with a trail on the left. Turn left and follow the trail, through thick chaparral, about 1/4 mile to the top of a ridge rising up from Red Box.

Follow the trail in a northerly direction, as it winds its way around Mount Lawlor on the right, to the saddle between Mount Lawlor and Strawberry Peak. From this point, the trail starts to descend the east side of the ridge. Leave the main trail, and follow a use trail to the north, along the ridge and over some ups and downs, then switchbacking steeply upward to the prominent summit of Strawberry Peak.

Notes:
Strawberry Peak is most comfortably hiked with canines during the spring and late fall, when the temperature is moderate. The hike can be rather sweltering during the summer months, and extra water should be carried.

According to Hiram Reid, who chronicled the early history of Pasadena and environs during the late 19th century, Strawberry Peak was affectionately named by "some wags at Switzer's Camp," because of the massive summit which, from various vistas, somewhat resembled a strawberry. Our favorite true story about Strawberry Peak took place in 1909 when the Grand Army of the Republic was sponsoring a week-long fair in Pasadena which offered, among the many amusements, balloon rides in Captain A.E. Mueller's giant gas balloon, *America.* One afternoon with high clouds overhead, Captain Mueller was taking the usual half-dozen passengers for a ride when, to the horror of the fair-going public, the balloon was snapped up by an air current and disappeared into the clouds. Reaching elevations as high as 14,000', the balloon and its terrified male passengers traveled through snow and rain. Just before nightfall, the Captain spotted grey boulders through the clouds and brought the balloon down upon the snowy summit of Strawberry Peak.

After spending a damp night huddled around a small fire trying to stay warm in the falling snow, the men wandered about the summit of the peak, looking off in every direction for some sign of life. They spotted a thin wisp of smoke coming from the chimney of a small snow-covered cabin some distance away. Greatly relieved in knowing that their predicament might soon end, they headed for the cabin through knee-deep snow. When they arrived at the cabin, they were greeted by early San Gabriel Mountain pioneers, Ma and Pa Colby, who dried their clothes and served them a hot meal while listening to their incredible story. The following day, Pa Colby led the group down the steep, snow-covered ridges to Switzer's Camp, where after a short rest, they made the long-awaited descent into the Arroyo Seco where family, friends, reporters and well-wishers waited. From the moment their hot-air balloon disappeared into the clouds above the San Gabriels, their story was front-page news across the country.

Vetter Mountain Lookout (5,908')
from Angeles Crest Hwy

Classification: easy
K9 water: 1/2 – 1 quart; no water on route
Suitable for small dogs or out-of-shape dogs
Though not posted, leashes are recommended
300' gain, 1.2 miles, 2 hours round-trip on fire road
Driving map:
Auto Club of Southern California: Los Angeles and Vicinity
Hiking map:
USGS Chilao Flat 7.5 minute topo
Best time to hike: April to November.
During the winter months, USFS road 3N16 is closed at Angeles Crest Highway. However, the road can be hiked from Angeles Forest Highway, but tends to be icy.

Driving:
Take I-210 to Angeles Crest Highway (2) in La Canada and exit. Drive north on Angeles Crest Highway approximately 23 miles to Charlton Flats Picnic Area, and turn left (USFS road 3N16). Drive 1.4 miles, staying left at all forks, to a gate across a dirt road (the paved road will continue on to the right). Park here, careful not to block the locked gate.

Hiking:
Walk around the gate and follow the dirt road to the summit of Vetter Mountain. There you will find a historic old fire lookout that is no longer used, but is in the process of being restored.
Hiking Variation:
There is a narrow use trail, which parallels the dirt road, that can be taken southeast from the summit along a ridge, back to the locked gate. The trail, which winds along the ridge through boulders, chaparral and pines, can be found behind some boulders just southeast of the summit.

Notes:
While you and your canine companion walk the dirt road to the summit, enjoy the smells of the Jeffrey and Ponderosa Pine, wild lilac, and mountain mahogany. The 360-degree view of the San Gabriel Mountains

Spectacular views from Vetter Mountain.

from the summit is absolutely spectacular. Vetter Mountain was named in the 1930s for USFS Forest Ranger Victor Vetter who was a recipient of the USFS Bissell Medal for his work in forest conservation. The fire lookout on the summit of Vetter Mountain was built in 1930.

Mt. Hillyer (6,200') from the Santa Clara Divide Road

Classification: easy
K9 water: 1/2 – 1 quart; no water on route
Suitable for small dogs
300' gain, 1.6 miles, 2 hours round-trip on fire road and trail
Driving map:
Auto Club of Southern California: Los Angeles and Vicinity
Hiking maps:
USGS Chilao Flat and Mt. Waterman 7.5 minute topos
Best time to hike: April to November
The Santa Clara Divide Road is often closed or blocked by snow during the winter months.

Driving:
Take I-210 to Angeles Crest Highway (2) in La Canada and exit. Drive north on Angeles Crest Highway approximately 26.5 miles to the Santa Clara Divide Road (USFS road 3N17) and turn left. Drive 2.8 miles on the Santa Clara Divide Road, past the signed entrance to the USFS Horse Flats Campground, about a half mile to a parking area on the left (west) side of the road. Walk to a dirt road just behind several wooden posts (which prohibit vehicular access to the dirt road).

Hiking:
Walk south on the dirt road which eventually narrows to a trail. Follow the trail up a small, steep hill through open meadows sparsely forested with Jeffrey Pine. The forest thickens somewhat, and large, prominent boulders mark either either side of the trail as it flattens out along the ridge to the summit. The summit of Mt. Hillyer is on the right (north) side of the trail, in the highest mound of rocks. A post marks the spot.

Notes:
The trail to Mt. Hillyer is a wonderful, peaceful trail shaded by pines, is off the beaten track, and is a popular hike for families with small children. An occasional rock climber can be found bouldering on the rocks near the summit of the peak.

Mt. Hillyer was named for Mary Hillyer (1865-1933) who worked for Angeles National Forest Supervisor William V. Mendenhall in the 1920's. The rocky outcrops of Mt. Hillyer and vicinity provided the perfect hideout for the bandito Tiburcio Vasquez (1835-1875), for whom Vasquez Rocks in Agua Dulce were named. The area now known as Horse Flats, below Hillyer's summit, was where Vasquez pastured his horses.

Off-leash, a well-trained trail dog will follow his master, won't chase wildlife, will not run up to other dogs or people who happen along the trail, and will respond immediately to his master's voice commands.

Mt. Williamson (8,214') from Angeles Crest Highway

Classification: moderate
K9 water: 1.5 quarts; no water on route
Suitable for small, well-conditioned dogs
1,600' gain, 5 miles, 3 hours round-trip on trail
Driving maps:
Auto Club of Southern California: Los Angeles and Vicinity
Hiking map:
USGS Crystal Lake 7.5 minute topo
Best time to hike: April to November.
During a heavy snow year, Angeles Crest Highway is often closed just past the Kratka Ridge ski area. Listed below are two alternate hiking routes up Mt. Williamson, one from the west and one from the east, which are accessed from two different trailheads/parking areas along Angeles Crest Highway.

Driving Route A:
Take I-210 to Angeles Crest Highway (2) in La Canada and exit. Drive north on Angeles Crest Highway approximately 38 miles to a large dirt parking area (about 2.5 miles past Kratka Ridge ski area) on the left (north) side of Angeles Crest Highway, about 1/2 mile before the first tunnel on the highway.

Driving Route B:
Take I-210 to Angeles Crest Highway (2) in La Canada and exit. Drive north on Angeles Crest Highway approximately 39.5 miles to Islip Saddle. Turn left into and park in a paved parking area on the North side of Angeles Crest Highway.

Hiking Route A:
From the east end of the parking lot, follow a dirt road about 100 yards to a trail and turn right (east). Follow this trail as it switchbacks up the southwest ridge of Mt. Williamson, through groves of Jeffrey and ponderosa pines. Approximately 2 miles up the trail, you reach the top of the ridge and the trail that comes up from Islip Saddle. From this point follow a use trail north, crossing several bumps to the summit.

Enjoying the top of Mt. Williamson. (PHOTO: Julie Rush)

Hiking Route B:
Start walking up the Pacific Crest Trail from the west end of the parking area. Follow the trail as it winds along the side of a mountain ridge which steepens steadily through open terrain, sparsely forested with pines and scrub. At the top of the ridge, turn right (northeast) on a use trail to the summit of Mt. Williamson, elevation 8,214'.

Notes:
Mt. Williamson was named after United States Army Lieutenant Robert Stockton Williamson who, in 1853, led a survey party charged with finding a suitable rail route across the San Gabriel Mountins. Williamson successfully located Cajon Pass and Soledad Pass.

From either route, this is a wonderful hike. From the summit, one can look out across the southern Mojave Desert. The boulder and rock out-croppings of the San Andreas Fault Zone can be seen running parallel along the base of the San Gabriel Mountains.

Mt. Lewis (8,396')

Classification: moderate
K9 water: 1/2 quart; no water on route
Suitable for small, well-conditioned dogs
500' gain, 1 mile,1 hour round-trip on use trail
Driving map:
Auto Club of Southern California: Los Angeles and Vicinity
Hiking maps:
USGS Crystal Lake 7.5 minute topo
Best time to hike: April to November, depending on snow.
During a heavy snow year, Angeles Crest Highway is often closed just
past the Kratka Ridge ski area.

Driving:
Take I-210 to Angeles Crest Highway (2) in La Canada and exit. Drive
north on Angeles Crest Highway approximately 44.5 miles to Dawson
Saddle on the left (north) side of the highway, where there is a highway
maintenance building. The name of the saddle is posted at the top of the
building. Park.

Hiking:
Just to the west side of the highway maintenance building is the use trail
to the summit of Mt. Lewis. Follow it, as it climbs steeply to the top of
the ridge, through groves of Jeffrey pines. At the top of the ridge, continue north to the summit of the peak.

Notes:
Mt. Lewis is a steep, short climb but well worth the spectacular views
across the Mojave Desert and the north side of the San Gabriel
Mountains. The peak was named after Washington "Dusty" Lewis, the
first Superintendent of Yosemite National Park and Assistant Director of
the National Park Service. As a topographer for the USGS, he worked
in the San Gabriel Mountains from 1906 to 1919 and was widely known
for his love of the wilderness. The summit of Mt. Lewis can be one of
the most rarely traveled, peaceful locations in the San Gabriel
Mountains

The Big Horn Mine

Big Horn Mine from Vincent Gap (6,565')

Classification: moderate
K9 water: 1 quart; snow-fed seeps and springs on route
Suitable for small, well-conditioned dogs
Though not posted, leashes are recommended
500' gain, 4 miles, 2 hours round-trip on dirt road
Driving map:
Auto Club of Southern California: Los Angeles and Vicinity
Hiking maps:
USGS Mount San Antonio 7.5 minute topo
Best time to hike: April to November, depending on snow.
During a heavy snow year, Angeles Crest Highway is often closed just
past the Kratka Ridge ski area.
Driving:
Take I-210 to Angeles Crest Highway (2) in La Canada and exit. Drive
north on Angeles Crest Highway approximately 46.9 miles to Vincent
Gap, and a large dirt parking area on the right (south) side of Angeles
Crest Highway. Park.

Hiking:
On the southwest side of the parking lot is a restroom, a trail sign (for
Mt. Baden-Powell and other trails) and a locked gate, painted red and
white. Take the dirt road on the other side of the locked gate (at the time
of this writing, there was no trail sign marking this route up to the Big
Horn Mine). Follow the road as it contours through tall pines across the
lower slopes of Mt. Baden-Powell. Continue up the road as it gradually
steepens. Nearing the top of the steep part, there is a road fork, marked
by a six-foot tall post on the right. On either side of this post are old
ruins and foundations of the turn-of-the-century mining camps. Continue on the road fork to the right, a short distance to the Big Horn Mine.
There is a cold snow-fed spring at the end of the road, coming out of the
closed mine. Recommend viewing the old mill site from this point.
Return by the same route.

Notes:
An interesting note about the rock formations found around the Big
Horn Mine. A combination of sea sediment and volcanics known as

Enjoying the wonders of the Big Horn Mine Trail.

Pelona Schist, these rocks were first deposited millions of years ago in the desert area south of the Blythe, California near the Colorado River. Remarkably, they were transported to the San Gabriel Mountains by movement along the San Andreas fault.

The Big Horn Mine, located in the Sheep Mountain Wilderness, was one of the largest gold mines in the San Gabriel Mountains, first prospected around 1895, by Charles Tom Vincent who lived in a cabin near Vincent Gulch. Unable to come up with the funds needed to run the mine, Vincent relinquished it to various promoters and mining companies who worked it intermittently over the next forty years or so.

The views along the trail to the Big Horn Mine are absolutely spectacular, across the deep canyon of the East Fork of the San Gabriel River to the dramatic peaks of the Mt. Baldy area. Mt. Baldy is often snow-capped in the months of April and May, and is a sight well worth seeing if you have the chance.

Sunset Peak (5,796')

Classification: moderate
K9 water: 1 quart; no water on route
Suitable for small, well-conditioned dogs
1,500' gain, 7 miles, 3 hours round-trip by dirt road
Driving map:
Auto Club of Southern California: Los Angeles and Vicinity
Hiking maps:
USGS Mount San Antonio and Mt. Baldy 7.5 minute topos
Best time to hike: all year, though the weather can be hot from June through September.

Driving:
Take I-10 to Indian Hill Blvd. in Claremont and exit. Drive north 2 miles on Indian Hill to Foothill Blvd. Turn right (east) on Foothill Blvd. and drive approximately 1 mile to Mills Avenue. Turn left (north) on Mills Avenue and follow to Mt. Baldy Road (which begins where Mills Avenue begins to turn northeast). Follow the Mt. Baldy Road approximately 7.8 miles to Glendora Ridge Road, located just on the outskirts of Mt. Baldy Village (if you go all the way through the village, you've gone too far). Turn left on Glendora Ridge Road and drive approximately 1 mile to the large dirt parking area on the right, known as Cow Canyon Saddle.

Hiking:
From the parking lot, walk south across the Glendora Ridge Road to a gated dirt road, somewhat hidden by chaparral. Walk the dirt road, as it parallels above the Glendora Ridge Road, while steadily climbing to the summit of Sunset Peak . There are two obvious forks on the dirt road. Stay left at each fork.

Notes:
The trail meanders up a fire road, through lush foliage which provides some nice, cool shade, though it can get quite hot during the summer months. From the summit of Sunset Peak are spectacular views of Mt. Baldy and on a clear day, the glistening Pacific Ocean and the summits of Santiago and Modjeska Peaks, the high points of Orange County can

On the shady trail to Sunset Peak.

be seen in the distance. In the 1920's, hikers from Camp Baldy named Sunset Peak after the Sunset Trail which passed below the peak, connecting Camp Baldy with Brown's Flat. There was once a fire lookout on the summit of Sunset that was built in the late 1920's, but only the concrete footings and some corrugated metal scraps are all that remain of it today.

4
The San Rafael Hills

Hundreds of thousands of years ago, the San Rafael Hills were actually attached to the San Gabriel Mountains, before earthquakes along the Sierra Madre fault zone pushed them to the front of the San Gabriel Range. A large valley, now known as the La Crescenta Valley, was formed between the two ranges. Flint Peak, the highpoint of the San Rafael Hills "towers" above Cerro Negro by only two feet and is almost three thousand feet lower than the lofty summit of Mt. Lukens, the highest point within the city limits of Los Angeles.

The San Rafael Hills are bordered by the great canyon of the Arroyo Seco to the east, Eagle Rock to the south and the Verdugo Hills to the west. Fires have always been part of the natural environment, but devastating ones swept across the San Rafael Hills during the late nineteenth century and first half of the twentieth century. During the depression years, the Civilian Conservation Corps (CCC) built a fire road along the crest of the San Rafael Hills. Using burros, the CCC also helped the USFS build fire stations on top of Mt. Lukens and Mt. Gleason. When the work was done, the burros were pastured in the fields and foothills surrounding the Crescenta Valley.

In November of 1933, a massive fire believed to be the work of an arsonist, began in the San Gabriel foothills above Tujunga, and quickly swept across the ridges and canyons surrounding Mt. Lukens. The fire burned more than a thousand acres and was fought by nearly three thousand men. The ensuing winter rains created disastrous flooding from the Big Tujunga Wash to the Arroyo Seco and canyons east. At least four hundred homes were lost and thirty-four known people died. As a result of that fire, the United States Forest Service built fire lookouts on the summit of Cerro Negro in the San Rafael Hills and on Mt. Verdugo in the Verdugo Hills. The tower on the summit of Mt. Verdugo has since been removed. Only the tower on Cerro Negro is still standing today, though it is no longer used as a fire lookout.

Old fire lookout on summit of Cerro Negro.

Cerro Negro (1,887')

Classification: easy
K9 water: 1/2 quart, no water on route
Suitable for small dogs or out-of-shape dogs
Though not posted, leashes are recommended
400' gain, 1.5 miles round-trip
Best time to hike: all year
Driving Maps:
Auto Club of Southern California: Los Angeles & Vicinity
Hiking Map:
USGS Pasadena 7.5 minute topo

Driving:
From Ventura Fwy, drive north on the Glendale Fwy 2. Exit on Mountain Street in Glendale. Drive east on Mountain which turns into Camino San Rafael. Follow Camino San Rafael as it winds through a residential area 1.9 miles to two fire roads on left. The north fire road (on the right) is paved and will be the one to hike. Park in the street, careful not to block the gate.

Hiking:
Walk up the paved fire road. The pavement ends about 500' from the gate. Go left at the first fork, passing by high power lines on the right. Pass homes on the right and continue on the fire road as it climbs uphill. Stay right at a second fork. The fire lookout will come into view. Follow road to fire lookout.

Notes:
The name "Cerro Negro" means Black Hill in Spanish. The San Rafael Hills are east of the Glendale Freeway, south of La Canada- Flintridge, north of Eagle Rock and west of Pasadena. The San Rafael Hills are much lower than the San Gabriel Mountains, yet have similar flora and fauna, though the effects of encroaching residential development can be seen. On a clear day, there are fabulous 360-degree views of the San Gabriel Mountains, La Crescenta Valley, Verdugo Mountains, the Los Angeles Basin and the Pacific Ocean from the summit. There is an old civil defense horn on the lookout tower. Volunteers from Jet Propulsion Laboratory's Amateur Radio Club keep the summit of Cerro Negro clear of brush all year long, especially during fire season.

"My passion is the dogs.

A lot of mushers really don't enjoy the wilderness
and the dogs as much as I do."

Susan Butcher, four-time winner of the 1,151 mile Iditarod,
The Last Great Race on Earth.

5

Hollywood Hills

Wilacre Park to Coldwater Canyon via the Betty B. Dearing Trail

Classification: easy/moderate
K9 water: 1/2 – 1 quart, no water on route
Suitable for small or out-of-shape dogs
Official City of Los Angeles dog park
500' gain, 2.5 miles, 1–2 hours round-trip
Best time to hike: all year
Driving Maps:
Auto Club of Southern California: Los Angeles & Vicinity
Hiking Map:
Not really needed – trail is well-marked.

Driving:
From the Ventura Fwy, exit on Laurel Canyon Boulevard and go south approximately 1.3 miles to Fryman Canyon Road. Turn right and park. The entrance to Wilacre Park is the first driveway on the right. This trail is very popular and on any given weekend, you'll find a lot of cars parked in every direction. It is a residential neighborhood, so be careful not to park in front of someone's driveway. More than one ticket has been issued and a car towed for blocking a driveway.

Hiking:
Walk up the paved driveway and follow the paved road as it gradually climbs up through the old cypress and jacaranda trees, to a plateau and the old foundation of what was once the estate home of Wil Acres, the cowboy movie star of silent motion picture fame. At this point, the pavement turns to a dirt fire road. Continue up the fire road as it winds its way around ridges. There are great views across the San Fernando Valley to the San Gabriel Mountains on a clear day. Follow the fire road to a major fork, marked by a Santa Monica Mountains Conservancy sign. Take the right fork (west) to Coldwater Canyon. About a hundred

yards from the fork, notice a stone stairway on the left. Follow this up a number of terraces to the TreePeople headquarters. If you miss the stairway, there is another one about a hundred feet down the trail in the direction of Coldwater Canyon. There are picnic tables, a restroom, a soda machine, and a faucet with a bucket beneath where people like to water their dogs. There is also an informational display, a recycling display and a nature trail. The TreePeople headquarters are open Monday through Friday (call for hours). Return to Laurel Canyon by the same route, downhill almost all the way.

Notes:

This hike can be done in reverse order, from the TreePeople parking lot to Laurel Canyon, or you can continue on to Fryman Canyon Overlook farther up the hill on Mulholland Drive, but we don't recommend this route for dogs for a couple of reasons. First, when we scouted the trail, it was very overgrown, to the point that we were having to pick our way through the thick brush. Having grown up in the Studio City hills, the author remembers how many rattlesnakes we used to catch in our backyard, and the idea of not being able to see below one's knees isn't a comforting thought when hiking in rattlesnake territory. We prefer the open fire road to the overgrown trail since the visibility is much better. The TreePeople is a non-profit group dedicated to tree-planting projects. Their headquarters are in the old Los Angeles County Fire Station 108, which was famous for pulling up the people who had the misfortune of driving off Mulholland Drive.

The trail was named for the late Betty B. Dearing who was active with the Santa Monica Mountains Conservancy.

Franklin Canyon Ranch Site

Classification: very easy to strenuous, small and out-of-shape dogs
K9 water: bring a bottle or bowl; there are water fountains
Posted: Dogs must be leashed and are not allowed in any water source
Best time to hike: all year
Driving Maps:
Auto Club of Southern California: Los Angeles & Vicinity
Hiking Map:
Trails are well-marked and NPS maps are available at the park

Driving:
From the Ventura Fwy 101, exit on Coldwater Canyon Boulevard and go south approximately 2.3 miles to Mulholland Drive. Turn right, not immediately onto Mulholland Drive West, but on the second street to the south, somewhat hidden by dense foliage. This is Franklin Canyon. Follow Franklin Canyon as it begins a winding descent through a residential neighborhood. At 0.2 mile, reach the park entrance. At 0.6 mile, turn left at fork with sign noting the Sooky Goldman Nature Center. At 0.7 mile, there is a parking lot on the left. Park here to walk around the lake or down to the Wodoc Nature Trail, or continue another 0.2 of a mile to a small parking area (room for maybe four or five cars) on the right, with restrooms. Park here for the beginning of the Wodoc Nature Trail. To get to the Doheny Ranch, continue down the road which crosses at the south end of a reservoir and turn right at the stop sign. Follow the road 0.3 miles and turn left on Lake Drive. Follow this about a half mile to a parking lot on the left with restrooms. There is a beautiful, large grassy area with picnic tables.

From Sunset Blvd., on the westside, go north on Beverly Drive which turns into Coldwater Canyon. Follow to Mulholland heading west. At intersection of Coldwater and Mulholland West, turn left on Franklin Canyon Drive.

Hiking:
This riparian area is filled with wildlife, including a variety of nesting birds, and is visited by families with small children, so it is important that pets are leashed. Pets are not allowed to swim in any body of water at the park, since the reservoirs are still actively used. In addition, canines frolicking in the water, will upset nesting wildlife.

Wodoc Nature Trail (0.1 mile): Easy nature trail, with interpretative signs identifying plants, that loops around Heavenly Pond (its real name), complete with a variety of ducks and a fountain. It is a favorite location for painting classes. Poopy scoop gloves are provided.

Chernoff Trail (0.6 mile): There are a number of different routes to take to walk around the lake. Some people just walk the road for ease. From the Wodoc Nature Trail, walk south along the paved road to the southeast end of the reservoir (note Cross Trail on opposite of road from this point). Follow the Chernoff Trail down along the water's edge, then walk through lush native and non-native plants. At the north end of the reservoir cross over to the west side (location depends upon height of water in reservoir) and continue around west side.

Cross Trail (0.7 mile, 200' gain): Cross Trail begins across the street from the southeast end of the reservoir as noted above. It climbs steeply for a short way, then essentially parallels Franklin Canyon, through coastal sage and chaparral. It ends at Franklin Canyon and Lake Drive. Another half mile down Lake Drive, and the Doheny Ranch is reached.

Hastain Trail (2.3 miles, 700' gain'): This is the most strenuous of the developed trails and starts just south of the ranch house on the east side of the lawn. Follow the trail as climbs steeply up a ridge, to an overlook with spectacular views out to the Pacific Ocean. From the overlook, follow the trail as it turns north (left) on the fire road and gently descends to the park entrance at Lake Drive.

Notes:

There are several other trails in Franklin Canyon and maps are usually available at trailside locations scattered around the park. The Doheny Ranch was one of six owned by the Doheny family, who made their fortune in the oil fields of Los Angeles around the turn of the century. The Spanish style house was built in 1935 at the north end of their four hundred acre Beverly Hills ranch and was used by the family as a weekend getaway. The upper Franklin Canyon reservoir was constructed in 1914 by the Los Angeles Department of Water and Power to store water transported down from the Owens Valley on the east side of the Sierra Nevada via the Los Angeles Aqueduct.

Sold to developers in 1977 who intended to build exclusive homes on the Doheny property, development was delayed for various reasons. The property was eventually purchased by the National Park Service in 1981 for the enjoyment of the public.

Bone-a-fido (!) Off-Leash Dog Parks, City of Los Angeles

Sepulveda Basin Off-Leash Dog Park
17550 Victory Boulevard, Encino CA 91316
Hours: sunrise to sunset, everyday
Located on the corner of White Oak and Victory Boulevards in the San Fernando Valley this is a safe and secure area where dogs can romp off-leash. It is the only park in the nation specifically developed for the purpose of letting dogs run unleashed. With plenty of parking, dog friendly amenities include mud-free water stations, pooper-scooper supplies, decorative fire hydrants and shade trees. The Sepulveda Basin Dog Park Fund has been established to enable pet lovers to make tax-deductible donations which will be used for improvements and maintenance at the park. To become a supporter of the dog park, call (818)785-5798.
Golden rules: Scat must be removed by owner; canines must be socialized - aggressive dogs are not allowed in the park; maximum of three dogs per person; all dogs must be over four months old, licensed and vaccinated; dogs with communicable diseases and females in heat must be kept at home; dogs must be leashed in the parking lot.

Silverlake Recreation Area
Silverlake Boulevard at Van Pelt Place in Silverlake
Hours: sunrise to sunset, everyday
Located on the south end of Silverlake Reservoir on Silverlake Boulevard a little over a mile from the intersection of Glendale and Silverlake Boulevards. A small stretch of grass which provides a place for pets to play in a crowded urban environment, this pilot dog park is a favorite haunt of all sizes and shapes of dogs especially on the weekends. The golden rules apply.

Wilacre Park aka Laurel Canyon Park
Laurel Canyon Boulevard at Fryman Canyon in Studio City
(see page 104 for description)
Hours: sunrise to sunset, everyday
One of the nicest places within the city where dogs can wander and sniff to their hearts content on trails that wind through chaparral country between the heart of Hollywood and the San Fernando Valley. The golden rules apply.

Bibliography

California Department of Fish and Game, *Living with California Mountain Lions,* California Department of Fish and Game, Sacramento, CA 1995

Carew, Harold D., *History of Pasadena and the San Gabriel Valley,* S.J. Clark Co, Pasadena, CA 1930

Harrison, Tom, *Trail Map of the Santa Monica Mountains, (Central and West)* Tom Harrison, San Rafael, CA 1993

Heil, Grant W., *The Ventura County Historical Quarterly,* Vol. XXI, No. 3, Ventura County Historical Society, Thousand Oaks, CA 1976

London, Jack, *The Call of the Wild and Other Stories,* Grosset & Dunlap, New York 1965

McAuley, Milt, *Hiking Trails of the Santa Monica Mountains,* Canyon Publishing Company, Canoga Park, CA 1991

Miller, Frances Trevelyan, *Byrd's Great Adventure,* The John C. Winston Company, Philadelphia, PA 1930

Muir, John, *Stickeen: The Story of a Dog,* Houghton Mifflin Company, New York 1916

Peters, Ed, *Mountaineering Freedom of the Hills,* The Mountaineers, Seattle WA 1982

Pomona Valley Humane Society, *Living with Wildlife,* Pomona Valley Humane Society, Pomona, CA 1995

Quirarte, Louis, *Summit Signatures,* Hundred Peaks Lookout, *Sierra Club,* Los Angeles, CA 1990

Robinson, John W., *Trails of the Angeles,* Wilderness Press, Berkeley, CA 1971

Rusho, W.L., *Everett Ruess: A Vagabond for Beauty,* Peregrin Smith Books, Salt Lake City, Utah 1983

Steinbeck, John, *Travels with Charley,* The Viking Press, New York 1962

United States Department of Agriculture, *Angeles National Forest Rules and Regulations,* Forest Service Pacific Southwest Region, USDA 1992

United States Department of the Interior, *Santa Monica Mountains National Recreation Area Eastern & Western Section maps,* National Park Service 1993

Wilkerson, Dr. James, A., *Medicine for Mountaineering,* The Mountaineers, Seattle WA 1985

Index